Institute of Classical Architecture & Art
20 West 44th Street, Suite 310, New York, NY 10036
Telephone: (212) 730-9646 Facsimile: (212) 730-9649
www.classicist.org

Guest Editors: Stuart Cohen and Julie Hacker

Managing Editor: Stephanie Salomon
Design: Suzanne Ketchoyian

ISBN: 978-1-7330309-0-8
ISSN: 1077-2922

ACKNOWLEDGMENTS

The ICAA, the *Classicist* Committee, and the Guest Editors would like to thank James Caulfield for his extraordinary and exceedingly generous contribution to *Classicist* No. 16, including photography for the front and back covers and numerous photographs located throughout this issue. We are grateful to all the essay writers, and thank in particular David Van Zanten. Mr. Van Zanten both contributed his own essay and made available a manuscript on Charles Atwood on which his late wife was working at the time of her death, allowing it to be excerpted and edited for this issue of the *Classicist*. We thank and appreciate the work of the anonymous peer reviewers. A special thank you is extended to Robert A.M. Stern for his astute advice and encouragement. Finally, we would like to thank the ICAA staff, particularly Mimi Bradley, without whom this issue would not have been realized.

Guest Editors Stuart Cohen and Julie Hacker are partners in the firm of Cohen & Hacker Architects and are the 2019 recipients of the Award for Excellence in Design, Academics and Scholarship given by the Society of Architectural Historians. For a biography of Stuart Cohen, see p. 49. Julie Hacker graduated from Wesleyan University and has an M.Arch. from the University of Illinois Chicago. A Fellow of the American Institute of Architects, she currently serves on the local and national boards of the AIA's Custom Residential Architects Network (CRAN). She also mentors young architects for the AIA and serves as a Preservation Commissioner for the City of Evanston, Illinois. She has been a frequent juror at schools of architecture and for AIA awards programs.

PHOTO CREDITS

Front cover: View looking south from Chicago's Michigan Avenue Bridge. Photo: © 2019 James Caulfield exclusively for the *Classicist*

Back cover: Michigan Avenue bridge house by Edward H. Bennett, 1918–20, framed by the Wrigley Building by Graham, Anderson, Probst & White, 1921. Photo: © 2019 James Caulfield exclusively for the *Classicist*

Front endpapers: Bird's-eye view of Chicago, 1860[?]. Library of Congress, Geography and Map Division

Page 63: Art Institute of Chicago by Shepley, Rutan & Coolidge, 1893. Interior detail. Photo: © 2019 James Caulfield

Page 79: Chicago Union Station by Graham, Anderson, Probst & White, 1925. Interior detail. Photo: © 2019 James Caulfield

Page 97: Chicago Cultural Center, (former Chicago Public Library) by Shepley, Rutan & Coolidge, 1893. Interior detail. Photo: © 2019 James Caulfield

Page 101: Shedd Aquarium by Graham, Anderson, Probst & White, 1930. Ceiling detail. Photo: © 2019 James Caulfield

Back endpapers: Daniel H. Burnham and Edward H. Bennett, Plan of Chicago, 1909, plate 87: "View Looking West Over the City, Showing the Proposed Civic Center, the Grand Axis, Grant Park, and the Harbor" (1907) by Jules Guerin, delineator. Watercolor and graphite on paper. Original held by the Art Institute of Chicago. Photo: Alamy Stock Photo

Printing: Allied Printing Services, Manchester, CT

CLASSICIST N° 16
CHICAGO

FOREWORD

In the Art Institute of Chicago there is a painting of youths in an Arcadian landscape by Pierre Puvis de Chavannes, once owned by Mrs. Potter Palmer, Chicago's first social doyenne. It displays an idealized classical landscape with a small lake and is entitled *The Sacred Grove, Beloved of the Arts and the Muses*. How different from the grim Chicago existing at the end of the nineteenth century with its vast stockyard and smoking mills, consuming waves of immigrants living nearby in deprivation, polluted by refuse of their own employment. With no organization to protect workers from exploitation, they fell victim to the industrial barons enforcing inhumane practices with private armies of security guards.

These same oppressors became the city fathers to the outside world, amassing and donating immense fortunes to establish civic enterprises such as schools, cultural institutions, and settlement houses. Their philanthropic generosity and business acumen attracted gifted and ambitious architects, for Chicago had become the fastest-growing city in the world after the devastating fire of 1871. Among others, Daniel Burnham and Louis Sullivan had been drawn to Chicago, where an architect's production was now measured in the lineal dimension of street frontage, not individual buildings.

As social unrest grew, the resident captains of industry on the South Side of the city relocated their families north of the Loop, away from the mills and stockyard, and their workers. Some moved even farther afield to newly organized suburbs such as Lake Forest, where roads abandoned the speculative grid for a more bucolic approach to domestic life in immense hidden estates of direct historical inspiration. Meanwhile, Oak Park and River Forest provided a more Emersonian vision of man in Nature conceived by Frank Lloyd Wright through his Prairie style.

Even in Arcadia, death prevails and the city fathers arranged for their final resting place in Graceland Cemetery. They imagined a private world, created precisely on the image of Puvis de Chavannes's *Sacred Grove*. Separated from the surrounding tenements by a brick wall, those who cherished the arts could mingle undisturbed for eternity. Visitors are transported by winding lanes through a native landscape, passing classical temples before glimpsing Potter Palmer's open temple protecting its two sarcophagi. In close proximity, a single Corinthian column identifies the tomb of George Pullman, the man who built an ideal town for his workers only to lower their wages and raise their rents. His body lies under a web of steel columns embedded in concrete for perpetual protection. In close adjacency is the powerful black granite Martin Ryerson tomb by Louis Sullivan, formed by the interpenetration of two unadorned mastabas, culminating in a pyramidical apex.

Barely visible on the opposite shore is found the astylar limestone Carrie Eliza Getty tomb, its battered walls delicately inscribed with an octagonal lattice. Monolithic slabs of limestone form the roof, and arched openings are outlined with shallow vegetative relief, while the gates and the recessed door are cast in bronze with ornamentation of transcendent beauty. The Getty tomb overlooks a small island in the lake, with a boulder marking the mute resting place of Daniel Burnham. On the adjacent bank, just below the Getty tomb, is found an inscribed gray granite slab marking the grave of Mies van der Rohe, while Louis Sullivan's is lost elsewhere in the wilderness of monuments.

Frank Lloyd Wright escaped Graceland and the cultural hegemony of the city in pursuit of a more populist path that led him back to the rural lands of his ancestors in Wisconsin. Tragedy of mythic scale unfolded there with his dreams consumed in a conflagration of epic proportion. Our dreams live on, but we are cautioned by these words of Mies, from an address given in 1950:

I hope you will understand that architecture has nothing to do with the invention of forms. It is not a playground for children, young or old. Architecture is the real battleground of the spirit.

—Thomas H. Beeby

Pierre Puvis de Chavannes, *The Sacred Grove, Beloved of the Arts and the Muses,* 1884/89 (detail), oil on canvas, 93 x 231 cm (36 7/16 x 90 15/16 in.). The Art Institute of Chicago, Potter Palmer Collection, 1922.445.

JOHN·B·MURPHY·MEMORIAL

LETTER FROM THE EDITORS

More than a single historical style, the classical tradition was understood as a coherent body of aesthetic thought that connected antiquity to the present via an unbroken chain of masterpieces. It offered a universal approach to design that celebrated balance, order, and harmony as the basis of beauty, and beauty as the measure of any successful design.
—Jonathan Mekinda, in *Art Deco Chicago*, ed. Robert Bruegmann, 2018

For many years the narrative of Chicago's architectural importance was defined by twentieth-century historians of modernism. It is equally true that assessments of the 1893 World's Fair and Chicago's contributions to the classical revival at the beginning of the twentieth century have been limited to discussions of the "City Beautiful" movement—the planning of building ensembles and the creation of civic spaces.

It was Daniel Burnham's genius to recognize classicism's potential to represent the aspirational nature of American society. While the World's Fair would introduce Americans to an idealized vision for the American city, the classicism of its buildings, despite their temporary nature, communicated the idea of longevity and permanence as an embodiment of the values of America's institutions. After the fair, Burnham and his new partners, Charles Atwood and Ernest Graham, modeled this through their classical buildings: city halls, courthouses, post offices, concert halls, and train stations built across the cities of this country. These buildings were immediately recognizable, as they are today, for their civic nature. This dissemination of classical architecture constitutes Chicago's important classical legacy.

From the 1890s on, beginning with the construction of the Chicago Public Library and the Art Institute of Chicago, the city's civic and commercial buildings were classical. In addition, from the turn of the century well into the 1930s, Chicago's architecture programs at both the School of the Art Institute and the Armour Institute, which taught joint classes, were modeled on that of the Ecole des Beaux-Arts. It was David Adler who recommended Mies van der Rohe for the directorship of the architecture program at the Armour Institute, soon to become Illinois Institute of Technology (IIT). While Mies's American work has been referred to as classical in its symmetry, axial planning, and purposeful emphasis on proportion, it was historian William Jordy's discussion of the symbolic content of this work that suggested that Mies may have had an agenda. This was arguably the invention of a universal language of classical architecture representing the elements of construction not as abstractions of trees, the human form, or wood construction, but utilizing the steel "I" beam as a twentieth-century icon of technology. It was reported that Frank Lloyd Wright said to Mies, upon seeing the plans for the IIT Library and Administration Building in 1944, "You know what you've done? Your have invented a new Classicism" (David Spaeth, *Mies van der Rohe,* 1985).

John B. Murphy Auditorium, Chicago, by Marshall & Fox, 1926, where The Driehaus Architecture Prize for excellence in classical architecture is awarded annually.

In Chicago today, classicism and traditional architecture exist primarily in the private realm. Recent townhouse construction has given Chicago's Near North Side new classical stone facades and influenced high-end residential developers. New high-rise apartment buildings continue to be predominantly concrete and glass. An occasional new building, however, recalls the elegant apartments designed by Benjamin Marshall in the 1920s.

Understanding the legacy of Chicago's classical architecture is the focus of this issue of the *Classicist.* The impact of the Chicago World's Fair, classicism's influence on Frank Lloyd Wright, the urbanism of Chicago's classical skyscrapers, Chicago schools that taught classicism, and the reintroduction of historical elements into Chicago design in the 1980s are all topics we have included. An enthusiasm for history and tradition in contemporary Chicago architecture may be seen in the professional portfolio that concludes the issue. It is our hope that this *Classicist* will help to further a dialogue about classicism here in Chicago.

—Stuart Cohen and Julie Hacker, Guest Editors

Photo: Courtesy of Antunovich Associates

CHARLES ATWOOD, DANIEL BURNHAM, AND THE CHICAGO WORLD'S FAIR

ANN LORENZ VAN ZANTEN

When John Wellborn Root, the designing partner of the Chicago firm of Burnham & Root, died suddenly of pneumonia in January 1891, Daniel H. Burnham despaired of replacing him. He wrote, "John's death has left a hole into which not one, but several strong men must be flung."[1] Yet he had to replace him, and soon he did, with a middle-aged New Yorker named Charles Bowler Atwood. Hired to work on the 1893 World's Columbian Exposition—the Chicago World's Fair—Atwood was made the chief architect of the fair by 1891. He played an important role in designing individual works and determining the overall appearance of the ensemble. In addition, he would soon be involved in the task of helping Burnham shift from his Romanesque style of the 1880s to a more discreet and urbanistically conscientious public and commercial style of architecture that was classically inspired.

Charles Atwood was born on May 18, 1849, in Charlestown, Massachusetts.[2] At age sixteen, he entered the architectural office of Elbridge Boyden in Worcester to learn drafting. The following year, he moved to Boston where he worked at the firm of Ware & Van Brunt, enrolling at the Lawrence Scientific School of Harvard University in the fall of 1869.[3] By the end of 1875, he was in New York City working as an architect for the interior decorating firm of Herter Brothers.[4] In 1878 or 1879, he worked on the plans for the lavish Fifth Avenue double residence of William H. Vanderbilt. The Vanderbilt houses were famous from the moment they were completed and were celebrated in a four-volume publication.[5] By 1885, they appeared, under Atwood's name as the designer, in a list compiled from choices by readers of *American Architect and Building News* of the ten best buildings in the United States. During this same period, Atwood began to try his hand at competitions. In 1884, he won a competition for the new Boston Public Library building.[6] The competition yielded twenty submissions, with Atwood awarded the first prize of $4,000. None of the submissions were judged suitable for construction and the commission for the library was eventually given to Charles McKim.

> "There has been nothing to equal it since the Parthenon."
> —Augustus Saint-Gaudens

By 1891, Daniel Burnham was enjoying the greatest coup of his already enormously successful career. Chicago was selected as the site of the 1893 World's Fair and Burnham was named chief of construction, with John Root assigned the role of consulting architect to the fair.[7] With this commission, Burnham was in a position not only to assert his presence on the Chicago architectural scene but also to ensure the national prominence of his firm. With the death of Root, Burnham immediately began looking for a new assistant, in the hope that he might also find a suitable design partner to join him in private practice after the fair.

Fig. 1. Fine Arts Building (now the Museum of Science and Industry) designed for the 1893 Chicago World's Fair by Charles Atwood (detail). Rebuilt as a permanent structure in the 1920s.

At this time, Atwood was building a small church in Manhattan and feeling terribly dejected about his prospects because of the financial depression beginning to sweep the country. Frederick Dinkelberg, with whom Atwood was sharing an office, mentioned that he had seen a notice of Root's death in the newspaper.[8] Dinkelberg encouraged Atwood to go to his old employer William Ware, by then head of the school of architecture at Columbia University, and ask his advice on how to get a position working on the World's Fair. Burnham later recalled that he received letters from both Ware and Bruce Price "calling my attention to Atwood and claiming for him the highest rank as an architect." When he consulted Charles McKim, though, "McKim shook his head in doubt."[9] Burnham nevertheless contacted Atwood and went to New York to meet him. Atwood missed their appointment but then followed Burnham back to Chicago and presented himself at Burnham's office. The exact date of these events is not recorded, but by April 21, 1891, Atwood had been hired as chief architect of the World's Columbian Exposition (fig. 2).

From a drawing by Thulstrup. Gibson Green/Alamy Stock Photo

Fig. 2. Daniel Burnham talking to Charles Atwood at his drafting table in the "shack," the temporary office for the 1893 Chicago World's Fair.

What moved Burnham to hire a man who had so quickly justified McKim's misgivings by missing his interview, then following him halfway across the country in desperate pursuit? Burnham himself supplied part of the explanation, writing about Atwood after his death, "Atwood was tall and rather slender, of elegant figure and bearing ... I often found myself marveling at his clearness and simplicity of statement, and the apt expressions which constantly issued from the mouth of this gifted man."[10]

Atwood must have had a remarkable presence and a deeply alluring personality, which had survived even the grief and disappointment of the death of his son and divorce from his wife in the late 1880s. It appears that Atwood easily must have fulfilled Burnham's ideal of the artistic type. It is clear from Burnham's relationship with Root that he needed as a partner someone who was not only a skillful designer but who behaved like an artist; that is, who was brilliant, tasteful, and a little unworldly, thus lending a certain tone of culture to Burnham's entrepreneurial skills while depending on Burnham for all the practical matters connected with actual commissions. It was this latter element of dependency that loomed larger after Root's death, for Burnham was no longer satisfied to have so full a partner as Root had been. He wanted final control of and final credit for the work of his firm, and this was undoubtedly easier to achieve when his design partner was, by Burnham's own account, "a mere child in the practical things of life." Sadly, those qualities that made Atwood attractive had a darker side that ultimately destroyed him.[11]

Atwood's further virtue, which went unmentioned, was that he represented the world that Burnham was anxious to become a part of. Successful and famous in his own right for the bold Romanesque buildings that he and Root had produced during the 1880s, Burnham nevertheless had obviously been electrified by the imposing classical designs presented by the East Coast architects attending the February meeting of the World's Fair designers. He was delighted by Augustus Saint-Gaudens's assertion that theirs was "the greatest meeting of artists since the 15th century," and he desired to be to be a full-fledged member of that company of Renaissance men.[12] As he told his biographer, Charles

Photo: From "Official Views of the World's Columbian Exposition: Issued by the Department of Photography." C. D. Arnold, Official Photographer. (Press Chicago Photo-Gravure Co., 1893)

Fig. 3. Fine Arts Building for the Chicago World's Fair, also called the Palace of Fine Arts, photographed in 1893.

Moore, about his selection of architects for the fair, "My scheme was to bring about men of the greatest experience. I was forty-four and one-half years of age and knew who the men were."[13] While Burnham had social status and a professional reputation, he had none of the formal European academic education enjoyed by most of his East Coast counterparts and no practice in designing in classical terms. Atwood provided an easy remedy for this situation.

As the principal designer working under Burnham's direction, Atwood was surely not a replacement for Root, who had been Burnham's intimate friend, but an employee who enjoyed his employer's complete confidence and often elicited his frank admiration. Burnham later wrote that after their initial meeting, he and Atwood had agreed that the latter would enter his private practice, but Burnham then decided that Atwood was most urgently needed on the World's Fair.[14] In his role as the fair's chief architect, Atwood was answerable to Burnham and to Ernest Graham, assistant chief of construction, who later would become a member of the D. H. Burnham & Company partnership that also included Atwood. Atwood's tasks were probably not very well defined, but he was responsible for reviewing the designs of architects contributing to the fair and seeing that they were ready for execution, and it was to him that the problem of designing a vast number of secondary buildings for the fair reverted. In this latter capacity he became the author of some sixty structures scattered about the exposition grounds. He was also certainly, if sometimes fortuitously, involved in important decisions about the ultimate appearance of the fair. For example, Graham wrote to Thomas Eddy Tallmadge in the 1920s that it was in a meeting at which he, Atwood, and Frank Millet were present that the decision was made to whitewash the buildings of the fair because there was not enough time to give them individual color treatment. Graham claimed that this meeting was the source of the idea for the white coloring of the fair, which became one of its most famous attributes.[15]

Atwood undoubtedly began at once to work on the secondary and unifying features of the World's Fair. His chance to prove himself on an equal footing with the fair's principal architects came abruptly in May 1891, about a month after he had taken up his duties.

Although early plans to use the lakefront just east of the Loop as an adjunct site for the fair had been abandoned on February 11, 1891, the question of whether a Fine Arts Building for the exposition, to be subsequently converted into a new Art Institute, might be erected on the lakefront continued to be debated throughout the late winter and early spring. As late as mid-April, it was still thought that the boards of the Art Institute and the exposition would join in financing construction of the design for an Art Institute, which John Root had made shortly before his death. On May 9, 1891, the *Chicago Tribune* ("Art Palace for the Lake Front") finally announced that while an exhibition building would be constructed at the lakefront, it would not be the fair's Fine Arts Building, but would serve to house the many congresses held to coincide with the exposition before being turned over to the permanent exhibit and teaching activities of the Art Institute. The job of designing it went to Shepley, Rutan & Coolidge of Boston, which had opened a Chicago office (to complete their work on the Chicago Public Library). It was at this point that it became apparent that yet another major commission for the fair was available in the form of an arts building. Burnham first offered the job to Francis Whitehouse, who was already working on the fair. When he declined on account of illness, Burnham turned to Atwood.[16] By that time, the matter was urgent; drawings for all the other major structures of the fair were already submitted and some had even gone out for bids. Atwood rose to the occasion. His design was completed by mid-June, and on June 17, the *Chicago Tribune* published an accurate drawing of the building.[17]

From *Vistas of the Fair in Color* (Chicago, 1894), The Art Institute of Chicago, Ryerson & Burnham Libraries

Fig. 4. The Chicago World's Fair's Fine Arts Building including the lions, which were relocated to the Art Institute building on Michigan Avenue.

But more important for Atwood's career than his quick response was the fact that his design won the unreserved admiration of his new employer. Burnham told Charles Moore in 1908, that the Fine Arts Building was "the most beautiful building I have ever seen."[18] And Burnham claimed that Augustus Saint-Gaudens had said, grasping him by the shoulders, "Do you realize the rank of Atwood's building among all the structures of the world? There has been nothing to equal it since the Parthenon."[19] In one stroke, Atwood had captured in the Fine Arts Building the flavor of the monumental classicism Burnham so admired and made it a symbol of the fair. In short, it embodied the best of all the buildings at the fair and the dream-like vision of a new classical civilization, which the "White City," as the fair came to known, represented in the public eye.

Burnham wrote that during preparations for the fair, Charles McKim remarked of Atwood's design, "Damn him, he is right every time."[20] In the context of the fair's supposedly exemplary architecture, Atwood chose to use precise details to heighten broad and largely original visual effects. The Fine Arts Building (also known as the Palace of Fine Arts) places a central dome on an essentially Greek building based on an 1867 Prix de Rome project done at the Ecole des Beaux-Arts by Emile Bénard for an art museum. Atwood's design introduces precisely this element. The strength of his arts building lies in the elements that are drawn neither from classical antiquity nor from

From *Vistas of the Fair in Color* (Chicago, 1894), The Art Institute of Chicago, Ryerson & Burnham Libraries

Fig. 5. Court of Honor at the at the Chicago World's Fair, illustration c. 1893. View east of The Grand Basin and the 65-foot gilded statue of "The Republic." Beyond is the Peristyle, a Corinthian colonnade, topped with 85 allegorical figures, and a triumphal arch at its center, designed by Charles Atwood.

From *Vistas of the Fair in Color* (Chicago, 1894), The Art Institute of Chicago, Ryerson & Burnham Libraries

Fig. 6. Chicago World's Fair, with the Agricultural Building (right) and the Atwood-designed Peristyle beyond.

recent Beaux-Arts design: the dramatic elongation of its repetitive surfaces and the crispness of its relationship to its site, with its two subsidiary pavilions creating a monumental forecourt to the north (figs, 3–6). Pressed tight against the edge of the North Pond, its steps descending directly into the water, the Fine Arts Building seemed at night to float like a ghostly antique island (figs. 1, 3, 4). This combination of monumentality and romance was itself the essence of the White City. It undoubtedly also delighted Burnham and contributed to his faith in Atwood's ability to carry over the ideals of the fair into private practice.

The Fine Arts Building was not Atwood's only success at the fair. On November 2, 1891, the Committee on Grounds and Buildings discarded the Casino in the lake and the thirteen columns, replacing them with Atwood's proposal for a Peristyle connecting a Music Hall, restaurant, and café, subsequently also referred to as the Casino.[21] The Peristyle's double colonnade included forty-eight columns, now representing all the states of the Union, with a statue over each one, the composition centering on a triumphal arch topped with quadriga. The whole ensemble, including the three-story pavilions at the ends, was 830 feet long. Like the Fine Arts Building, the Peristyle was a highly praised feature of the fair. It seems to have been based on the widely published Palais Longchamp in Marseille, designed by Henri Espérandieu in 1862. Atwood adapted the composition, flattening its exedral form and rendering it in a Roman Baroque style more suitable to the fair (figs. 5, 6).

Fig. 7. Reliance Building, Chicago, designed by Atwood for D. H. Burnham & Company, 1894.

The success of these and Atwood's other works at the fair, such as the railroad Terminal Station, the Forestry Building, and numerous smaller structures, left Atwood in a professional position that he had not enjoyed since the completion of the Vanderbilt houses. He was awarded medals for his work alongside the established East Coast and Chicago architects of the main buildings, and his Fine Arts Building was repeatedly referred to as the best building in the exposition.

Rewarded with professional and social recognition, Atwood, more importantly, assumed a position of authority in Burnham's practice. On March 1, 1894, Atwood was made a partner in the newly incorporated D. H. Burnham & Company with a share of 27 percent of the firm's profits, surpassing the 10 percent shares given to Ernest Graham, office superintendent, and Edward Shankland, engineer and overseer of plans and construction.[22] While not a full successor to John Root in his personal relations with Burnham, Atwood was nonetheless firmly established as the resident artist that Burnham needed to complement his own role as masterful organizer and entrepreneur.

Even before Atwood became a partner, he was heavily involved in the affairs of Burnham's firm. As early as March 1892, well over a year before he left the position of chief architect of the Chicago World's Fair, Atwood was designing commercial buildings for Burnham. It was his work on the fair that brought Atwood wide public acknowledgment, but the designs he made for Burnham's private practice, such as the Marshall Field Annex Building in Chicago and the Ellicott Square Building in Buffalo, New York, were more important for the course of Burnham's architecture and its shift to classicism at the end of the nineteenth century. While Atwood remains largely unknown, his design for the Reliance Building (fig. 7) for Burnham is now illustrated in almost every major history book on the development of twentieth-century architecture.

The late **Ann Lorenz Van Zanten** was appointed the first Curator of Architecture at the Chicago Historical Society (now Chicago History Museum) in 1982. This article is published courtesy of David Van Zanten and was excerpted and edited by Stuart Cohen from an unpublished manuscript for a book on Charles Atwood.

Notes

1. Daniel Burnham, quoted in Thomas S. Hines, *Burnham of Chicago: Architect and Planner* (Chicago: University of Chicago Press, 1979), 90.

2. Charles Atwood obituary, *Chicago Times-Herald,* December 20, 1895.

3. *List of Students of the Lawrence Scientific School, 1847– 1894* (Cambridge, MA: n.p., 1898).

4. Arthur Woltersdorf, "A Portrait Gallery of Chicago Architects: III, Charles B. Atwood," *Western Architect* 33, no. 8 (August 1924). Atwood does not appear in New York directories until 1880, when he was living at 105 E. 18th Street.

5. See W. A. Croffut, *The Vanderbilts and the Story of Their Fortune* (Chicago and New York: Bedford, Clarke, 1886); and Edward Strahan, *Mr. Vanderbilt's House and Collection,* 4 vols. (Boston, New York, and Philadelphia: George Barrie, 1883–84).

6. For the history of the competition, see Walter Muir Whitehill, *The Boston Public Library, A Centennial History* (Cambridge, MA: Harvard University Press, 1956); and Horace G. Wadlin, *The Public Library of the City of Boston: A History* (Boston: Trustees of the Public Library of the City of Boston, 1911).

7. *Final Report of the Director of Works of the World's Columbian Exposition* (Chicago: n.p., 1894). See also Hines, *Burnham of Chicago*; and Henry N. Higginbotham, *Report of the President to the Board of Directors of the World's Columbian Exposition, Chicago, 1892–1893* (Chicago: Rand McNally & Co., 1898).

8. Woltersdorf, "A Portrait Gallery of Chicago Architects: III, Charles B. Atwood."

9. Charles Moore, *Daniel H. Burnham: Architect, Planner of Cities,* vol. 2 (New York: Houghton Mifflin Co, 1921), 48. Burnham mentions the letters from Ware and Price in the obituary he wrote of Atwood, "Charles Bowler Atwood," *Inland Architect and News Record* 26, no. 6 (January 1896): 56.

10. Burnham, "Charles Bowler Atwood."

11. Atwood was frequently depressed, and by the time he was in Chicago working for Burnham he had become a heroin addict. Atwood's presence in the firm became more unreliable and Burnham finally had to dismiss him. Atwood's early death may have been a suicide or a heroin overdose, prompted by his dismissal.

12. Charles Moore, *Daniel H. Burnham,* 47. See also Daniel Burnham, interview by Charles Moore, 1908, typescript held at the Burnham and Ryerson Libraries, Art Institute of Chicago.

13. Burnham, interview by Moore.

14. Ibid. Charles Moore writes in *Daniel H. Burnham* (48), "Mr. Atwood became chief designer for Mr. Burnham's private work. The demands of the Fair, however, became so insistent that he was compelled to give up the private work."

15. Thomas E. Tallmadge, *The Story of Architecture in America* (New York: W. W. Norton & Co., 1927), 204–05.

16. Charles Moore. *Daniel H. Burnham,* 49. See also *Final Report of the Director of Works of the World's Columbian Exposition.*

17. "Plans for the Art Palace," *Chicago Tribune,* June 17, 1891.

18. Moore, *Daniel H. Burnham,* 48, and Burnham, interview by Moore.

19. Burnham. "Charles Bowler Atwood."

20. Burnham, interview by Moore. In *Daniel H. Burnham* (49), Moore writes, quoting Burnham a bit differently, "He [McKim] spent one entire afternoon looking over Atwood's drawings. Every little while he took down the books, looked at them and then, turning to me would say: 'Confound him, he is right every time.'"

21. See "There Will Be No Casino. Two Additional Fair Buildings in its Stead," *Chicago Tribune,* November 3, 1891; and "Chicago," *American Architect and Building News* 34, no. 830 (November 21, 1891): 119.

22. Donald Hoffmann, *The Architecture of John Wellborn Root* (Baltimore: Johns Hopkins University Press, 1973), 182, n. 19.

CIVIC OPERA BUILDING

THE "BEAUX-ARTS BOYS" OF CHICAGO

AN ARCHITECTURAL GENEALOGY, 1890–1930

JEANNE SYLVESTER

Before the first architecture program was founded at the Massachusetts Institute of Technology (MIT) in 1868, Americans who wanted to study architecture in an academic setting went to the Ecole des Beaux-Arts in Paris. The curriculum of the Ecole focused intensely on classical architecture and influenced the training of generations of American architectural students beginning in the 1840s. When MIT—and later Columbia University, in 1881—established their schools of architecture, they both employed faculty and pedagogy from the Ecole. Classicism as taught by the Ecole and instilled in architectural students proved to be so popular that "Beaux-Arts" became a distinct style of architecture and an influential movement in twentieth-century American architectural history. The Beaux-Arts style in Chicago began with the 1893 World's Columbian Exposition, also known as the World's Fair.

Chicago's most successful architect at the time was Daniel H. Burnham, and he and his partner John Root were named supervising architects of the World's Fair. Burnham was appointed director of works and was in charge of choosing the architects to design the buildings. Desirous that the fair be viewed as a national and not just local event, and at the same time keenly aware that the artistic and architectural reputation of Chicago was at stake, Burnham approached leading architects from the East Coast to solicit their involvement. While the architects were initially reluctant to participate, Burnham convinced the group that they would be building a "dream city" that would influence the future of American architecture. Burnham and the other architects agreed that the fair should be designed in one cohesive classical style, with buildings bearing a common cornice line, thus ensuring a harmonious composition.

Fig. 1. Chicago Civic Opera Building (Civic Opera House) by Graham, Anderson, Probst & White, 1929.

The chief architects of the fair were Richard Morris Hunt, Charles Follen McKim and Stanford White of McKim, Mead & White, and George Browne Post, all from New York; Henry Van Brunt and Frank Maynard Howe, of Van Brunt & Howe, originally from Boston but later from Kansas City; and Robert Swain Peabody and John Stearns of Peabody & Stearns, from Boston. All were influenced by Hunt, who was the first American graduate of the Ecole, president and co-founder of the New York Society of Architects, which became the American Institute of Architects, and founder of the Society of Beaux-Arts Architects. Of those remaining architects, McKim, Peabody, and Howe studied at the Ecole; Post worked in Hunt's office; and Post and Van Brunt trained in the Beaux-Arts atelier that Hunt developed. Facing criticism from the Chicago architectural community for hiring only East Coast architects, Burnham later added William Le Baron Jenney and William B. Mundie, Henry Ives Cobb, Solon S. Beman, and Louis H. Sullivan and Dankmar Adler.

> Along with D. H. Burnham & Company, three other firms dominated the design of classical buildings in Chicago.

The organizers of the fair emulated the Paris Universal Exposition of 1889, which featured a Court of Honor framed by monumentally large exposition buildings. All but Cobb's and Adler & Sullivan's buildings were classical in design, and of those Chicago architects who designed for the fair, only Beman's was placed on the Court of Honor. Thus, the influence of the East Coast architects, whom Burnham called the "Beaux-Arts Boys," dominated. Burnham's respect for their work and his friendship with Charles McKim resulted in Burnham's emergent admiration for the classical style, and Burnham's success and powerful presence influenced generations of architects in Chicago and throughout the country.

Burnham was recognized for his accomplishment in planning the fair, and in 1909 he published the Plan of Chicago with Edward H. Bennett (a graduate of the Ecole). Without question the single most influential planning document in American urban planning history, the Chicago Plan is a direct expression of the City Beautiful movement, which incorporated civic order and rational arrangements of buildings, monuments, long vistas, and open spaces in a hierarchical manner along major and minor axes according to function.

Fig. 2. Marshall Field department store (now Macy's) by D. H. Burnham & Company 1892. Interior detail.

Beaux-Arts buildings were typically monumental in feel and embellished with classical ornament. Skyscrapers were designed in the Beaux-Arts style using a classical column for reference, and their facades were divided into three separate and distinct elements following a classical column's base, shaft, and capital, with applied classical ornament.

Burnham's firm enjoyed the success resulting from the fair and the Plan of Chicago, going on to design a significant number of notable buildings in Chicago and across the country, most in the classical style. Along with D. H. Burnham & Company, three other firms—Graham, Anderson, Probst & White, Burnham's successor firm; Holabird & Roche; and Shepley, Rutan & Coolidge—dominated the design of classical buildings in Chicago constructed between 1893 and the Great Depression. A brief genealogy of these firms follows.

D. H. BURNHAM & COMPANY

Daniel Burnham

Daniel Burnham (1846–1912) failed his entrance exams at Harvard and Yale, although later, in recognition of his success, both universities awarded him honorary degrees. He became a draftsman for architect and engineer William Le Baron Jenney, and later joined the firm of Carter, Drake & Wight, where he met John Wellborn Root. The two formed Burnham & Root, one of the nation's preeminent architectural firms. Together they designed the Montauk Building (1893), the Rookery Building (1888), the Monadnock Building (1892), and the Masonic Temple (1892), among others. After Root's death in 1891, Burnham hired Charles Atwood as a replacement. In 1894, Burnham reorganized his firm and named Charles Atwood consulting architect and, for a short while, chief designer, with Ernest Graham as junior partner.

Designs by D. H. Burnham & Company for Chicago include the Marshall Field department store (1892, with an annex done with Charles Atwood, 1907; fig. 2); the Illinois Trust & Savings Bank (1896);

planning for the Field Museum of Natural History (1893); the Merchants Loan & Trust Company Building (1900); the Railway Exchange (Santa Fe) Building (1904); Orchestra Hall, now the Chicago Symphony Center (1904); the Heyworth Building (1904); an addition to the Carson Pirie Scott Store (1906); the Peoples Gas, Light, and Coke Company Building (1911); the Insurance Exchange Building (1912); the Reid Murdoch Building (1914); and the Continental and Commercial National Bank Building (completed by Graham, Anderson, Probst & White in 1914). Outside of Chicago, the firm designed, among other buildings, Union Station in Pittsburgh (1898), the Frick Building in Pittsburgh (1902), the Flatiron Building in New York (1902), Union Station in Washington D.C. (1907), Selfridges in London (1909), Wanamaker's Department Store in Philadelphia (1911), and Filene's Sons Company Building in Boston (1912).

Almost two hundred employees worked for Burnham. Of those, several notable architects continued designing in the classical tradition in Chicago and elsewhere in the country, including Karl M. Vitzthum, Frederick Dinkelberg, Peter Weber, and Willis Polk.

Fig. 3. Chicago Union Station by Graham, Anderson, Probst & White, 1925. Interior detail.

Charles B. Atwood

Charles Atwood (1849–1895), who attended the Lawrence Scientific School at Harvard University, is credited with the design of the original Vanderbilt double house in New York. He designed more than sixty buildings for the Chicago World's Fair, including the Palace of Fine Arts (1893; today the Museum of Science and Industry, rebuilt from the temporary fair building), which is often considered the most successful design of all of the buildings, and is the only structure still standing on its original site. While working for Burnham, Atwood designed the Reliance Building (1894–95; see p. 14) and the Fisher Building (1895–96), both with simplified neo-Gothic ornamentation.

Karl M. Vitzthum

Karl Vitzthum (1880–1967) graduated from the Royal College of Architecture in Munich. Vitzthum worked for Burnham and for Graham, Anderson, Probst & White, and later joined John Burns, a graduate of Washington University in St. Louis. Vitzthum & Burns designed several significant Beaux-Arts-influenced buildings, including the Bell Building, now the Old Republic Building (1925); the Hyde Park-Kenwood National Bank Building (1927–28); the Midland Club Building, now the W Chicago Hotel City Center (1927); and the Steuben Club Building (1929), now the Randolph Tower City Apartments.

Frederick P. Dinkelberg

Frederick Dinkelberg (1858–1935) studied architecture at the Pennsylvania Academy of the Fine Arts in Philadelphia. He worked on the World's Fair and later with D. H. Burnham & Co. designing the Santa Fe Building (1903-04; today the Railway Exchange Building), which contained Burnham's offices and later the offices of Burnham's successor firms; the Heyworth Building; the Commercial National Bank Building (1907); and the Conway Building, now known as the Burnham Center (1914). In 1918, Dinkelberg formed his own firm with Joachim G. Giaever, a structural engineer, and was the principal designer for the Jewelers Building (1925–27), now known simply by its address, 35 East Wacker Drive.

Peter J. Weber
Born in Germany, Peter Weber (1863–1926) was educated in Berlin at the Charlottenburg Institute. He was an assistant to Charles Atwood on the World's Fair, and while employed by Burnham in Chicago he worked on a number of buildings, including the Illinois Trust and Savings Bank, the Silversmith Building (1896), and the Fisher Building.

Willis W. Polk
Willis Polk (1867–1924) studied at Columbia University and worked with McKim, Mead & White and Bernard Maybeck before working with Burnham in Chicago. Polk established and directed Burnham's San Francisco office and designed the Merchants' Exchange Building (1904) and the glass curtain-walled Hallidie Building (1917).

GRAHAM, ANDERSON, PROBST & WHITE

Ernest Graham
Ernest Graham (1866–1936) joined Burnham in working on the World's Fair in 1891. Like Burnham, the Michigan-born Graham, who received technical training at Coe College and later at the University of Notre Dame, admired the work of the "Beaux-Arts boys from the East," and the firm's designs during the period they worked together through Burnham's death in 1912 were unabashedly and exuberantly neoclassical. Graham was Daniel Burnham's sole junior partner from 1898 until 1910 when Burnham's sons, Daniel Jr. and Hubert, joined the firm. Burnham and Graham's collaboration was not only prodigious; it also made the architectural firm one of the most successful in the nation.

Fig. 4. Field Museum of Natural History by Graham, Anderson, Probst & White, 1921. Interior detail.

In 1908, Burnham and Graham reorganized the firm, placing Graham in charge of business and overseeing (William) Peirce Anderson, head of design, Edward Probst, head of plans, and Howard J. White, in charge of superintendence. When Burnham died in 1912, the firm was reorganized as Graham, Burnham & Company and practiced for five years until the Burnham brothers left to form their eponymous firm, and Graham formed a partnership with Anderson, Probst, and White. Graham, Anderson, Probst & White proved to be arguably the most successful firm in Chicago that designed in the classical tradition and applied Beaux-Arts planning principles to its designs.

Peirce Anderson
(William) Peirce Anderson (1870–1924) graduated from Harvard College, attended Johns Hopkins University for a postgraduate course in electrical engineering, and later studied at the Ecole des Beaux-Arts. With Anderson as head of design, it can safely be said that every building by the firm of Graham, Anderson, Probst & White either originated with Anderson or was overseen by him.

Edward Probst and Howard J. White
Edward Probst (1870–1942) had no formal architectural education and began as an apprentice, working at various architectural firms until he joined Burnham in 1898. Howard White (1870–1936) attended the Chicago Manual Training School before he became a draftsman at Burnham & Root.

Notable designs by Graham, Anderson, Probst & White in the classical tradition in Chicago include the

Insurance Exchange Building (1912, with an addition in 1928); the Stevens Building (1913); the Continental and Commercial National Bank Building (1914); the Field Museum of Natural History (1921; fig. 4); the Federal Reserve Bank (1922); the Wrigley Building (1921; see p. 47) and its north annex (1924); the Straus Building (1924); Chicago Union Station (1925; fig. 3); the Builders' Building (1927); the Pittsfield Building (1927); the National Life Insurance Company Building (1928); the State Bank of Chicago Building, (1928); the Chicago Civic Opera House (1929; fig. 1); and the Shedd Aquarium (1930). Outside of Chicago, principal works of the firm include the Equitable Building in New York (1915); the U. S. Post Office in Washington D.C. (1914, with an addition in 1933); the Cleveland Terminal Group (1930); the Gimbel Brothers Building in Philadelphia (1927); and the Thirtieth Street Station in Philadelphia (1934).

Graham, Anderson, Probst & White was the largest architectural firm during the early twentieth century. Extant records of the firm identify only a few names of draftsmen, among them Theodore Lescher, George Robard, and Edward Bennett, who attended the Ecole des Beaux-Arts and worked with George Post. Other draftsmen who had significant careers were Charles Beersman, Alfred Shaw, Sigurd Naess, Mario Schiavoni (Shedd Aquarium), and Charles Murphy.

Charles G. Beersman
Charles Beersman (1888–1946) studied architecture at the University of Pennsylvania and joined Anderson's firm in 1919. He participated in designing the Federal Reserve Bank, the State Bank of Chicago, the Builders' Building, the Foreman State National Bank Building, the Straus Building, and Chicago Union Station. Beersman was the primary architect under Peirce Anderson responsible for the design of the Wrigley Building.

Fig. 5. Monroe Building by Holabird & Roche, 1912. Interior detail.

Alfred P. Shaw
Alfred Shaw (1895–1970) studied architecture at the Boston Architectural Club atelier. He became head of design at Graham, Anderson, Probst & White after Anderson died and completed Chicago Union Station to Anderson's designs, in addition to the Pittsfield Building, the Chicago Civic Opera House, and the Merchandise Mart (1928–30). Shaw respected classical architecture, but he brought a more streamlined aesthetic to the firm, and under his leadership and with the help of his assistant Sigurd Naess, the firm's designs were transformed into the simplified modern forms of Art Deco. Shaw later formed a firm with Naess and Charles Murphy.

HOLABIRD & ROCHE

Another prominent firm that designed classically influenced buildings was Holabird & Roche. William Holabird (1854–1923) studied at West Point and moved to Chicago to work for William Le Baron Jenney. Martin Roche (1853–1927) also worked for Jenney without formal architectural training. Holabird & Roche designed buildings for the Chicago World's Fair, and while they later became known for their skyscrapers, they also designed smaller classical buildings. Among the firm's many achievements are the Marquette Building (1895), the Arthur T. Aldis House (1895), the University Club of Chicago (1908), the Cook County Courthouse (City Hall, 1910), the Monroe Building (1912; fig. 5), the Lumber Exchange Building (1915), the Chicago Temple Building (1923), Soldier Field (1924), and the third Palmer House Hotel (1925).

Significant architects who worked with Holabird & Roche include E. A. Renwick, the firm's third partner after Holabird and Roche, and Oskar Wehle, who later partnered with William J. Dodd. Wehle and Dodd designed numerous classical buildings throughout the Midwest. F. J. Thielbar was superintendent of construction at Holabird & Roche until 1918 and lead designer of the Chicago Temple Building. He later partnered with John Reed Fugard, and together they worked with Giaever and Dinkelberg as supervising architects on the Jewelers Building.

Other architects who worked for Holabird & Roche include Frank B. Long, chief draftsman, who graduated from the University of Illinois, and who went on to form a partnership with Frederick Kees that was responsible for the design of several significant classical buildings in Minnesota. Charles E. Fox studied architecture at MIT and left Holabird & Roche in 1905 to join Benjamin Marshall in forming Marshall & Fox. Notable classical designs for Chicago by Marshall & Fox are the South Shore Country Club (1905), the Blackstone Hotel (1909), the Drake Hotel (1919), and the John B. Murphy Auditorium (1926; see p. 6), built for the College of Surgeons and now the site of the award ceremony for The Driehuas Architecture Prize for classical architecture.

Fig. 6. Chicago Cultural Center, formerly the Chicago Public Library, by Shepley, Rutan & Coolidge, 1893. Interior detail.

Fig. 7. Chicago Cultural Center.

SHEPLEY, RUTAN & COOLIDGE

In 1892, the Boston-based firm of Shepley, Rutan & Coolidge—the successor firm that formed after the death of Henry Hobson Richardson—won a competition to design the Chicago Public Library (1893), now the Chicago Cultural Center (figs. 6, 7). A year later, the firm designed the "palace of culture" that was to serve as a meeting hall for the World's Fair and is now the Art Institute of Chicago, as well as the Ryerson and Burnham Libraries (1901) and McKinlock Court (1924) at the Art Institute.

Charles Coolidge (1858–1936) studied at both Harvard College and MIT. He was familiar with Chicago, having supervised the construction of Richardson's Glessner and McVeagh houses. In 1915 the firm, which included George Shepley (1860–1903) and Charles Rutan (1851–1914), opened an office in Chicago where Coolidge partnered with head draftsman Charles Hodgdon. Known for its designs of educational buildings, Coolidge & Hodgdon designed about a dozen buildings for the University of Chicago in the Collegiate Gothic style, including Swift Hall, Joseph Bond Chapel, William Rainey Harper Memorial Library, and Ida Noyes Hall, as well as the classical Tenth Church of Christ Scientist in Hyde Park.

The legacy of Daniel Burnham and the 1893 World's Columbian Exposition was the inspiration of generations of architects whose designs imbued the city with a rich built heritage. For almost four decades, the civic, institutional, and commercial buildings designed by these men formed the classical face of not only Chicago architecture but architecture throughout the country. Burnham famously captured this, as quoted in "Stirred by Burnham, Democracy Champion" in the *Chicago Record-Herald* on October 15, 1910:

Make no little plans; they have no magic to stir men's blood … Make big plans; aim high in hope and work, remembering that a noble, logical diagram once recorded will never die, but long after we are gone will be a living thing, asserting itself with ever-growing insistency. Remember that our sons and grandsons are going to do things that would stagger us. Let your watchword be order and your beacon beauty.

Jeanne Sylvester is the founder and managing member of Sylvester Historic Consultants, LLC. She has documented numerous properties for the Historic American Building Survey, including Chicago Union Station, prepared several successful Illinois Historic Property Tax Assessment Freeze Applications for Susan Benjamin of Benjamin Historic Certifications, and drafted reports documenting the history and architecture of multiple buildings on the University of Chicago campus. Sylvester received a B.A. in history from Northwestern University and a J. D. from DePaul University College of Law, and recently earned an M.S. in Historic Preservation from the School of the Art Institute of Chicago.

A special thanks to Len Koroski of Goettsch Partners, Sally A. Kitt Chappell, and the three anonymous peer reviewers.

Sources include:

Bruegmann, Robert. *The Architects and the City: Holabird & Roche of Chicago, 1880–1918.* Chicago: University of Chicago Press, 1997.

———. *Holabird & Roche/Holabird & Root: An Illustrated Catalog of Works 1880–1940.* New York: Garland Publishing, in cooperation with the Chicago Historical Society, 1991.

Chappell, Sally A. Kitt. *Architecture and Planning of Graham, Anderson, Probst and White, 1912–1936: Transforming Tradition.* Chicago: University of Chicago Press, 1992.

———."As if the Lights Were Always Shining: Graham, Anderson, Probst and White's Wrigley Building at the Boulevard Link." In Zukowsky, John, ed. *Chicago Architecture, 1872–1922: Birth of a Metropolis.* Munich: Prestel, in association with The Art Institute of Chicago, 1987.

Chicago History Museum. Holabird & Root Collection, accession no. 1792.242, Ledgers, Box 1.

Graham, Ernest. *The Architectural Work of Graham, Anderson, Probst & White and Their Predecessors D. H. Burnham & Co. and Graham Burnham & Co.* London: B. T. Batsford, 1933.

Hines, *Thomas S. Burnham of Chicago: Architect and Planner.* New York: Oxford University Press, 1974.

Miller, Donald L. *City of the Century: The Epic of Chicago and the Making of America.* New York: Simon & Schuster, 1996.

Noffsinger, James Philip. "The Influence of the Ecole des Beaux-Arts on the Architects of the United States." PhD diss., Catholic University of America, 1955.

Van Roessel, Annemarie. *D. H. Burnham and Chicago's Loop.* Chicago: The Art Institute of Chicago, 1996.

Zukowsky, John, ed. *Chicago Architecture and Design, 1923–1993: Reconfiguration of an American Metropolis.* Munich: Prestel. 1993, in association with The Art Institute of Chicago, 1993.

A MUSEUM

TEACHING CLASSICISM IN CHICAGO, 1890–1930

ROLF ACHILLES

With the opening of the Illinois and Michigan Canal in 1848, Chicago saw exponential growth in the areas of transportation, industry, and population. After the Civil War, the city's stockyards became a commercial juggernaut led by such business trailblazers as Philip Armour. The flood of poor European immigrants into the city helped fuel the feverish domestic and commercial building activity after the Great Chicago Fire of 1871, which would lead to the innovations that spotlighted Chicago on the world's architectural stage.

Even while Chicago was experiencing unprecedented growth, in 1886, fewer than 100 architectural degrees were awarded in the United States by what were the three established architecture schools—the Massachusetts Institute of Technology (MIT, 1868), Cornell University (1871), and the University of Illinois (1867). By the spring of 1886, the general consensus among architects throughout the Midwest was that practitioners in Chicago and farther west were no longer looking only to the East Coast for architectural ideas, but were originating designs of their own, and that there was a need for an architecture school in Chicago. Civic boosters, architects, and contractors saw no reason why Chicago should not also be a center of architectural education, and members of the Illinois State Association of Architects held meetings in Chicago to address the question of architectural instruction.

While not coming to specific conclusions, these meetings affirmed the need for formal training for architects.

Fig. 1. Paul Durbin McCurry (American, 1903-1991), *Student Project, Junior Year Design Project at Armour Institute of Technology*, 1924, graphite pencil, ink, and watercolor on watercolor paper; 95.2 × 59.5 cm (37 7/16 × 23 7/16 in.). The Art Institute of Chicago, gift of Paul McCurry, 1983.899.

Dankmar Adler and Normand Smith Patton suggested that the Chicago Architectural Sketch Club was ideally suited for the establishment of an architecture school in Chicago modeled after the traditional French Beaux-Arts style. Adler's main concern was cost, and he speculated that "at least $25,000 a year would be required." Chicago Architectural Sketch Club members Patton, Henry W. Will, and George Beaumont formed a committee to look into the matter.[1]

Early in 1889, the Chicago Woman's Club requested that "in the formation of the contemplated architectural school, there should be no distinction between sexes, and that students of either sex should be admitted."[2]

Of the university architecture programs, only MIT's was headed by an academically trained architect, William R. Ware, who had spent a year at the Ecole des Beaux-Arts. Cornell's Charles Babcock had earned a B.A. before

> Civic boosters, architects, and contractors saw no reason why Chicago should not also be a center of architectural education.

he received his architectural training in the offices of Richard Upjohn. Nathan Ricker, upon being awarded a degree in architecture, was immediately appointed head of the Department of Architecture at the University of Illinois. Even with an architecture school already established downstate, in Champaign, Chicago's leading supporters saw another opportunity in the newly named Art Institute of Chicago (AIC). Its stated mission was to be "a school of art and design," dedicated to "the formation and exhibition of collections of objects of art,

Fig. 2. Art Institute of Chicago, 1904.

Fig. 3. Armour Institute of Technology, c. 1900.

and the cultivation and extension of the arts of design by any appropriate means."[3] Charles L. Hutchison was appointed its president, Alfred Emerson its curator of classical antiquities, and William Merchant Richardson French (brother of the sculptor Daniel Chester French) its director.

French had come to Chicago in 1867 as a Harvard-educated engineer, but gained a national reputation for his lectures and articles on art. In 1878, he became secretary of the Chicago Academy of Design which was, a year later, reorganized as the Chicago Academy of Fine Arts and changed its name again, to the Art Institute of Chicago, in 1882. French served first as its secretary and then its director, from 1885 until his death in 1914.

With what became known as the School of the Art Institute of Chicago (SAIC) flourishing, several of the Chicago Architectural Sketch Club's lectures kept the issue of an architectural school in Chicago alive. On July 1, 1889, R. A. Dennell presented a paper titled "Architectural Students." It received wide attention when it was published in *Inland Architect* in September of the same year.[4] Dennell outlined a course of study that might take "four to eight years." He also carefully crafted a statement suggesting that to become an architect required both formal study and actual practice rather than just an apprenticeship.

Already in SAIC's *Tenth Annual Report*, published in June 1889, it had been noted that "the departments of modeling and decorative designing, which were introduced four years ago [headed by Louis J. Millet], are now fully established and doing excellent work. A department of architecture will next urge itself upon our attention, and there are encouraging elements in the interest of the architectural societies and private architects. While it would be impossible to open a comprehensive school of architecture without a considerable endowment, it may be possible to establish certain classes for architectural students at the Art Institute this fall."[5] With support from the Illinois State Association of Architects and other groups, the Art Institute of Chicago announced that "with the beginning of the new school year, Monday, September 23 [1889], classes in architecture will be opened as a part of the regular course of the art school."[6]

There seem to be no surviving records for the classes offered that first year, or the number of students attending. Existing records for the Department of Architecture start with the year 1891–92.

The Art Institute catalogue for the following school year, 1892–93, names two women and twenty-four men enrolled in the Department of Architecture and states that they were accorded the same privileges as art students. The intent of the new department, which also called itself the Chicago School of Architecture, was to offer technical instruction at moderate cost to the student of architecture, the draftsman, and the designer.

The founding faculty consisted of Louis J. Millet for architecture and design; Walter F. Shattuck for mathematics and architecture; William A. Otis as lecturer on history of architecture; W. S. MacHarg as lecturer on sewerage and ventilation; Irving K. Pond as lecturer on theory of design; William Le Baron Jenny as lecturer on construction; and Miss C. D. Wade (and other teachers in the art school) for free-hand drawing, watercolor, and pen and ink. William French lectured to the architecture students as well.

Millet also was the founding director of the Department of Decorative Designing, in 1889, when he was asked to additionally serve as director and then dean of the new Department of Architecture. His joint appointment lasted until 1901–02. Millet was a proponent of "pure design," which proposed teaching composition before historical precedents with the intent that the study of

Fig. 4. Architecture class, Chicago School of Architecture, 1898.

Fig. 5. Design class, Chicago School of Architecture, 1895.

precedents would then lead to the identification of architectural principles.

From its start, the department's catalogue announced that this was a two-year program, which also offered classes three evenings a week and Saturdays, and that a drafting room would be accessible at all times. Evening classes were "available to draftsmen and other persons engaged in the actual practice."[7]

The 1891 catalogue outlined the architecture program as follows. The first term of the first year encompassed mathematics, geometry, and descriptive geometry; architecture with an emphasis on the study of the five orders, and readings in the history of architecture; and a third course focused on freehand and instrumental drawing as well as lettering.

The second term again included mathematics but with a focus on descriptive geometry, plane trigonometry, and logarithms. There was another class on the history of architecture and a studio on "original architectural problems." The required drawing course concentrated on freehand and instrumental drawing with the addition of instruction in watercolor.

Fig. 6. First-year student project by Robert Bacon, Chicago School of Architecture, 1898–99.

The third term of the first year featured mathematics and descriptive geometry. The lectures on architecture were devoted to the theory of design. There was also a design studio dedicated to problems and a class in drawing covering freehand and instrumental drawing and watercolor.

The first term of the second year brought students mathematics with a concentration on perspective. Architecture now focused on general construction, materials, foundations, and superstructures. The drawing class again stressed freehand and instrumental drawing and watercolor.

The second term of this year once more featured mathematics with a focus on perspective. The class on architecture included instruction in specifications and estimating. There were also lectures on general construction in addition to a design studio. Pupils studied the history of ornament with prescribed readings. The drawing class repeated freehand and instrumental drawing and gave instruction in pen-and-ink and watercolor.

The third-term architecture course continued the study of specifications and estimating, with lectures on general construction, ventilation, and sewerage. The design studio focused on the design of ornament.

This two-year day program was full-time, providing a comprehensive class schedule that effectively eliminated the possibility of students working even part-time in architectural offices. With the completion of the library, SAIC boasted an extensive collection of new books and photographs for student use.

The Department of Architecture's published catalogue did not specifically state that the school had a stylistic focus, however, from its first published illustrations of student work, projects were classically inspired, especially by the buildings of the Chicago World's Fair. By 1905, there were renderings and floor plans of domestic spaces, theaters, an occasional skyscraper, and even a gas station. Even while the 1902–03 catalogue proclaimed that Chicago, "by force of its position is one of the most potent influences in the development of American architecture,"[8] the published drawings did not reflect the now-acclaimed commercial architecture that students saw daily in Chicago's Loop.

In 1890, Chicago minister Frank Wakely Gunsaulus delivered what came to be known as the "Million Dollar

Sermon" from the pulpit of his South Side church. In it he said that with a million dollars he could build a school where students could learn to think in practical not theoretical terms—where they could be taught to "learn by doing." Inspired by Gunsaulus's ideas, Philip Danforth Armour gave Gunsaulus one million dollars with which to establish the Armour Institute. Armour, who ran his family's meat-packing enterprise, saw the founding of a namesake institute as a way to fill his need for skilled engineers and technicians. When the Armour Institute opened in 1893, with Gunsaulus as its president, it offered professional courses in engineering, chemistry, architecture, and library science in its own five-story fireproof building at the corner of Armour Avenue and 33rd Street.

Throughout the nineteenth century, architecture was considered a fine art and it was taught as such. As a department within a school and museum devoted to fine art, SAIC's Department of Architecture was unique, but the faculty also realized that architecture was both an art and a science. To this end, an alliance with the Armour Institute was seen as natural and symbiotic. This partnership furnished both schools with resources in their respective strengths. SAIC's architecture students could use Armour's laboratories for courses in electrical, mining, and mechanical engineering, much of which had direct application to architectural study.

In 1893, the Art Institute moved into its new building along Michigan Avenue facing Adams Street. It had been built for the World's Columbian Exposition and was designed by Charles A. Coolidge from the Chicago office of the Boston-based firm Shepley, Rutan & Coolidge. In the new spaces, AIC set up permanent rooms and facilities for the school and its departments.

In 1894, Americans who had studied at the Ecole des Beaux-Arts in Paris founded the Beaux-Arts Society

Fig. 7. Student project, design for an Academy of Fine Arts by Alfred S. Alschuler, Chicago School of Architecture, 1900–01.

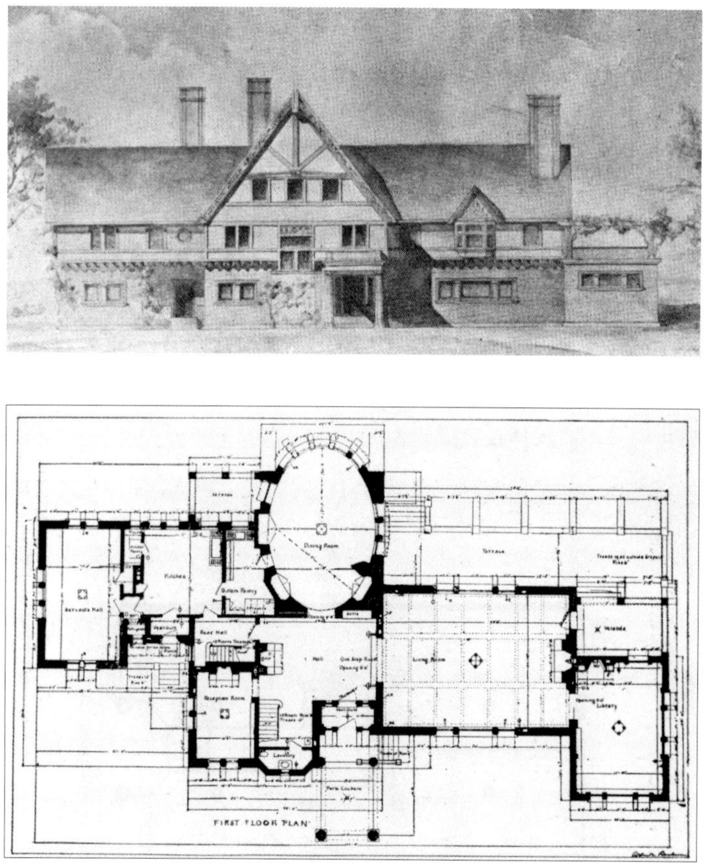

Fig. 8. Student project, elevation and plan for a suburban house by Adelaide Benham, Chicago School of Architecture, 1901–02.

of Architects (renamed in 1912 the Society of Beaux-Arts Architects which, in turn, in 1916 evolved into the Beaux-Arts Institute of Design) in New York City to promote the educational activities and principles taught in Paris. The Society quickly set up evening classes

Graduates of the Art Institute's Chicago School of Architecture and the Armour Institute . . . became the backbone of Chicago's great firms.

across the United States for working architects to learn Beaux-Arts design. It supplied the written programs for studio projects and student competitions used by most of America's university-based architectural programs. Chicago had its first Beaux-Arts atelier by 1900, with several other ateliers opening within the decade.[9] The Society's yearbooks included competition entries from Chicago with the names of studio instructors, suggesting that its competition programs were used by the School of the Art Institute.

In 1894, SAIC's Department of Architecture adopted a four-year program allied with the Armour Institute. This course load resembled the architecture courses offered by several East Coast schools. At the same time, the department retained its two-year program of shorter courses resembling those of schools in Boston and New York. It also kept its evening and Saturday programs as options. For the first school year of its new alliance with Armour (1894–95), with rooms in the AIC's new building, the Department of Architecture had thirty-two students, including two women.

In 1898–99, the SAIC classrooms were enlarged by the addition of a new building with a skylit study room. The designation "Special Course" was established to meet the needs of students who had neither the time nor the means to devote four years to the study of architecture. Two years of special work was rewarded with a certificate. To connect the School of Architecture more closely with the architectural profession and to aid the students with counsel and critiques, a Board of Advisors made up of practicing architects was formed in 1900. The first board was composed of Daniel H. Burnham, Charles A. Coolidge, Charles S. Frost, J. Gamble Rogers, and Howard Van Doren Shaw, with Alfred F. Granger joining in 1901. This committee apparently did not approve of Louis Millet's "pure design" classes and had enough sway that for the academic year 1902–03, Victor C. Alderson was named dean of the Chicago School of Architecture, returning the curriculum to the study of classical precedents.

During the four-year course of study, classes were arranged so that the technical subjects were studied in the morning at the Armour Institute, while the afternoon sessions were devoted to drawing and purely architectural study and conducted at the Art Institute. Admission to the program presupposed that a student had acquired a knowledge of the use of drawing instruments and of geometrical drawing in a preparatory school or in an architect's office. When a first-year class had completed two or three designs, one of the city's prominent architects, usually from the Board of Advisors, critiqued the finished work and awarded citations and mentions for the best work, in the Beaux-Arts tradition.

In their second year, students started to make perspectives of all their designs. This was a valuable exercise for three-dimensional thinking. Also, from their second year on, students learned about masonry, soils, metals, sanitation, heating and ventilation, and carpentry, as well as the history of architecture. With their instructors, students visited manufacturers of building materials, and inspected buildings under construction as well as completed ones. These visits augmented textbook readings with direct on-site experience. Students made freehand drawings from the Art Institute's extensive collection of architectural casts, which had been originally exhibited at the World's Columbian Exposition.

From 1902 through the academic year 1916–17, the Department of Architecture enrolled about 100 students annually. There were few women among them. By 1916, there were nearly twenty schools offering formal training to architects in the United States, almost all, like the Art Institute, following the system developed by the Ecole des Beaux-Arts in Paris.

In 1918, SAIC was reorganized and the study of architecture was reduced to one class in architectural design

Fig. 9. Student project, design for a concert hall by Harry B. Aarens, Chicago School of Architecture, 1915–16.

Fig. 10. Student project, design for a church and parish house by Harold Smith, School of the Art Institute of Chicago, Department of Architecture, evening class, 1917–18.

taught by an MIT graduate with a year of experience at the Ecole des Beaux-Arts. The evening architecture class was taught by Charles D. Faulkner, of the Armour Institute. Earl H. Reed Jr., with a B. S. from MIT, taught architectural design. Armour and SAIC continued their alliance, but the reorganized Chicago School of Architecture published a separate catalogue stating that all questions about curriculum and enrollment were to be directed to the Armour Institute. From 1919 on, SAIC students were graduated from the Armour Institute of Technology.

For another two decades, graduates of SAIC's Chicago School of Architecture and the Armour Institute were still classically trained. These graduates became the backbone of Chicago's great firms, among them D. H. Burnham & Company; Graham, Anderson, Probst & White; and Holabird & Root.

In hindsight, it is ironic that SAIC's Department of Architecture, providing a classical education, was called the Chicago School of Architecture—a name that would later become synonymous with Chicago's "progressive" steel-frame construction, and a term that Chicago historian Thomas Tallmadge applied to the city's acclaimed commercial architects. A further irony was David Adler's recommendation of Ludwig Mies van der Rohe to head the Armour Institute in 1938. Mies converted the curriculum to the study of "modern," architecture, although, one could argue, a modernism that was classically inspired.

Rolf Achilles is an art and architecture historian with a special interest in Chicago. He is on the board of directors of the Richard H. Driehaus Museum, and the Hegeler Carus Mansion. He is also an Honorary Freeman of the Worshipful Company of Glaziers and Painters of Glass in London, and was awarded Freedom of the City of London in 2013. Achilles lectures nationally and internationally and is widely published on several platforms.

Notes

1. Wilbert R. Hasbrouck, *The Chicago Architecture Club: Prelude to the Modern* (New York: The Monacelli Press, 2005), 90

2. Chicago Architectural Sketch Club, "Association Notes," *Inland Architect* 13, no. 4 (April 1889): 60; also cited in Hasbrouck, *The Chicago Architecture Club*, 90.

3. *Art Institute of Chicago Catalog* (Chicago, 1897), 6.

4. R. A. Dennell, "Architectural Students," *Inland Architect* 14, no. 2 (September 1889): 22.

5. School of the Art Institute of Chicago, *Tenth Annual Report*, June 1889.

6. "Instruction in Architecture," *Inland Architect* 14, 2 (September 1889), 23.

7. *The Art Institute of Chicago, Circular of Instruction* from 1891 and subsequent catalogues describe the rooms available, and the expanding library and photograph collection.

8. *School of the Art Institute of Chicago Catalog*, Circular, 1902–03, 59.

9. Hasbrouck, *The Chicago Architecture Club*, 385ff.

FRANK LLOYD WRIGHT AND BEAUX-ARTS DESIGN

DAVID VAN ZANTEN

Any consideration of Chicago architecture would be incomplete without a discussion of Frank Lloyd Wright and the time he spent working in Chicago. While he would become an outspoken critic of historical eclecticism, his early work shows the influence of Chicago's Beaux-Arts architectural milieu. —Stuart Cohen and Julie Hacker

After visiting the United States in 1911, H. P. Berlage wrote in the *Schweizerische Bauzeitung*, "I don't know whether Sullivan studied in Paris, but Wright is a student of the Ecole des Beaux-Arts."[1] A number of very intelligent contemporary observers, encountering the work of Frank Lloyd Wright around the time of the publication of his 1911 *Ausgeführte Bauten*, reacted similarly. Le Corbusier, for one, wrote to his friend H. T. Wydeveld in 1925, "One senses in the plans of Wright the good teaching of the Ecole des Beaux-Arts here [in Paris], that is to say, an attention to order, to organization, to the character of pure architectural form."[2] We know from Wright's *Autobiography* (1932, second edition 1943) that when Charles Atwood left Daniel Burham's office, Burnham offered first to send Wright to the Ecole, then a place in his office—to which Wright responded, "It's too late now I'm afraid. I am spoiled already. I've been too close to Mr. Sullivan"[3] (Sullivan had been trained at the Ecole). Colin Rowe years later remarked to Chicago architectural historian Kevin Harrington, echoing his friend and teacher Henry-Russell Hitchcock, that this was because Wright was already the best "Beaux-Arts" architect in Chicago.

Did Wright—like so many of his contemporaries in America—learn something from Paris? Certainly the dominating cross-axial spaces of his George Blossom House of 1892 (figs. 1, 2) would make one think so—not to mention its categorically classical decorative vocabulary. The Blossom House we can visit and we find all the spaces of the ground floor opening to each other—not through square openings but through broad archways producing a much more dramatic play of architectural form. Wright seems to be seeking something already suggested in his Beaux-Arts-trained teacher Louis Sullivan's very compressed Charnley House of 1890. Later in the 1890s, Wright transformed this geometric play into one of octagonal spaces in his plans for the Devin and McAfee houses and his executed George Furbeck House in Oak Park (1897; fig. 3).

Fig. 1. George Blossom House, Chicago, by Frank Lloyd Wright, 1892.

These houses are neither modern nor revivalist, as we have been made to understand them. What might have been going on? I think to answer this question we must

Did Wright—like so many of his contemporaries in America—learn something from Paris?

first ask what really constituted the famous "Beaux-Arts" approach.[4] In the abstract it was a technique of sequential design elaboration starting with an idea and ending with a delineated spatial form. This pivoted on certain selections among choices of shape and relationship obliging the designer to take a general philosophical stand visible as a graphic pattern. Only in final elaboration would this be adjusted to emerge in three dimensions with section and elevation, a pictorial-spatial manifestation of the origi-

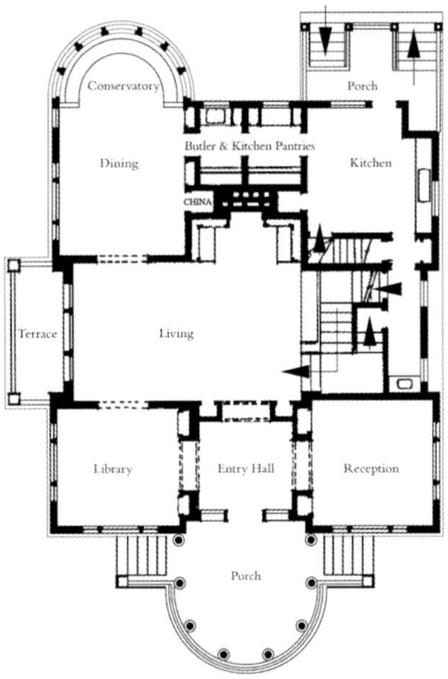

Fig. 2. George Blossom House. First-floor plan.

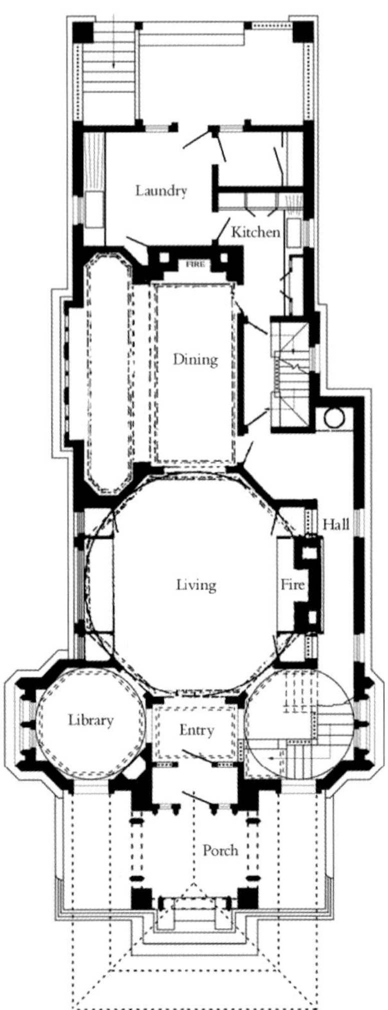

Fig. 3. George Furbeck House, Oak Park, Illinois, by Frank Lloyd Wright, 1897. First-floor plan.

nating idea. The value of the Beaux-Arts system consequently lay in that it was conceptual, generating a solution from a problem rather than applying some ready-made "model"— stylistic or functional—which might "fit."

Instructional texts specified how the student was to proceed: from the "elements" of architecture (rooms and courtyards, corridors and stairways, doors and windows) to their arrangement—their "composition"—as a building. This was a test of ordering and logic. The student was to start with a quick reading of the program to grasp its spirit, then a slower and attentive reading to grasp the details (the school programs being carefully written to aid such analysis), then a quickly thrown-off mass of sketch plans testing as many arrangements—"partis"—as possible. (In the Grand Prix competition this was specifically to be done in twelve hours.) Last came the famously detailed final carpet plans (in the Grand Prix competition rendered, with help, in four months).[5] Julien Guadet, a professor at the Ecole des Beaux-Arts, put it very simply: the student divides the problem into its constituent parts, selects one as the characterizing dominant, then "proceeding from the whole to the parts, from the building masses to their details, you proceed effortlessly," but, he warns, "if your point of departure has been well-chosen."[6] The outside, thus, manifested the inside; the inside was transparent to the parti. This parti was the most minimal sketch idea settled on at once after the intense analysis—and because of the conceptual nature of this exercise, it determined whether the building was a good or bad design.

One of the last French Beaux-Arts teachers in America, Jean-Paul Carlhian, liked to remark that this method was clear thinking and clear exposition, as one was taught in lycée. Edouard Arnaud in 1928 compares it to the game of chess: "This intellectual work is comparable to that involved in a chess problem. In both cases one seeks a solution based, not on fixed principles, but [on] an imaginative suggestion aided by a solid working method."[7] But this was all a matter of the plan. The elevations—as was all too often observed—were all too similar and predictably "classical" in vocabulary. The plans made up for this predictability by their extraordinary intricacy and intertwining, the deciphering of which became like following a subtle game or exploring a complex pattern.

Fig. 4. Milwaukee Public Library Competition entry (top, preliminary; bottom, final) by Frank Lloyd Wright, 1892.

What were the tangible results of this Beaux-Arts method? In Wright's archive (recently catalogued at Columbia University's Avery Drawings and Archives Collection) we find two classical competition schemes for the Milwaukee Public Library of 1892: one working off Perrault's west facade of the Louvre, the other off Emile Bénard's celebrated 1867 Grand Prix project already the inspiration of Charles Atwood's Fine Arts Building at the World's Columbian Exposition, although for Wright's library we lack a plan, which is the core of Beaux-Arts composition (fig. 4).[8] Another American example of Beaux-Arts from the years we are discussing might be a library design submitted in 1892 for what became the 42nd Street Central Building of the New York Public Library by Ernest Flagg (fig. 5).[9] Here we see Flagg first privileging the stack blocks in three wings extending from a domed central link, then fixing the reading space divided into four octagonal volumes projecting on the diagonals at the crossing. But was this all there was to Beaux-Arts design? It

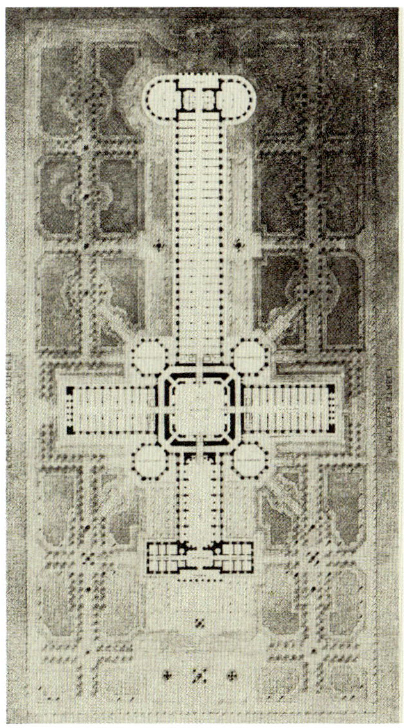

Fig. 5. Plan for the New York Public Library by Ernest Flagg, 1892.

is interesting to compare this declarative solution to that of a leading French designer establishing himself in the United States, Paul Philippe Cret, who handles this more adroitly in his Indianapolis Public Library of 1914–20 in their common selection of the book check-out space as the central feature and in their centrifugal layering of circulation, stacks, and window-lit reading spaces around it. The layout is similar but the result dramatically different, and that lies in Cret's tight joining of the spaces and their access to light (fig. 6). The difference between Flagg and Cret's plans is that between the literal and the metaphorical, between student work and architecture. The point in design, Cret wrote, presenting this design in his article "Library Architecture" in the twelfth edition of the *Encyclopedia Britannica*),[10] is to divide the problem into its spatial parts—here we would understand the catalogue and check-out space, book stacks, reading rooms, and entry and corridor spaces—then to select the one most immediately characteristic and characterizing—the "point" in Beaux-Arts parlance—then arrange the remaining parts symmetrically but subordinately around it—that Gestalt, the composition's commitment or "*parti.*" In the case of the American big-city public library, he continued, the borrowing of books rather than their reading on site was the central activity so that, by Beaux-Arts logic, the catalogue and check-out space should dominate the composition with reading spaces subordinate around it.

What was the source of Wright's Beaux-Arts plans? Here . . . we have to note the presence of Louis Sullivan . . .

Yet perhaps we are missing the point. Flagg sees this problem as one of geometric play. His "building" is only a drawing, and as such it is fascinating even though, had it been executed, it would have been labyrinthine and frustrating—like a Beaux-Arts project but also like the plan of Wright's Furbeck House of 1897, spinning sub-spaces off the diagonals of an octagonal central space—although at a vastly smaller scale.

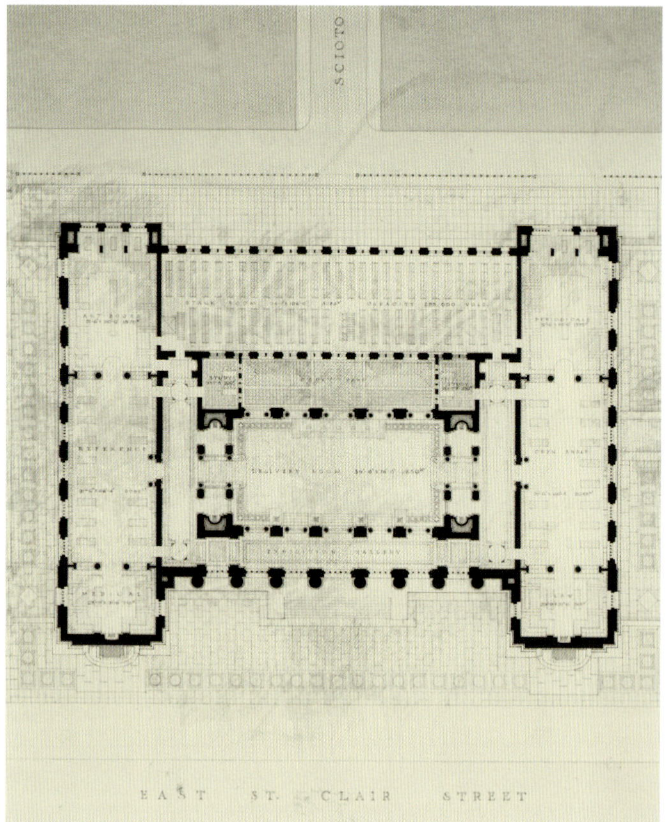

Photo: Paul Philippe Cret papers, Kislak Center for Special Collections, Rare Books and Manuscripts, University of Pennsylvania

Fig. 6. Competition plan for the Indianapolis Public Library by Paul Philippe Cret, 1914.

What was the source of Wright's Beaux-Arts plans? Here I think we have to note the presence of Louis Sullivan—winner of the French prize at Boston English High School and trained in the Beaux-Arts system, first by Eugène Letang at MIT in 1872–73, then at the Ecole itself as a student of Letang's teacher, Emile Vaudremer, in 1874–75. What might Sullivan have learned in Paris? He denied that it was the literal program of the Ecole, writing in his *Autobiography of an Idea*, "He familiarized himself thoroughly with the theory of the School, which, in his mind, settled down to a theory of the plan, yielding results of extraordinary brilliancy, but which, after all, was not the reality he sought, but an abstraction, a method, a state of mind that was local and specific—not universal."[11] This, perhaps, is just the point.

An incident, repeated twice: Louis Sullivan presenting himself formally, lecturing to an audience and stating his idea of architecture, once before the newly founded Western Association of Architects in 1886; and again in

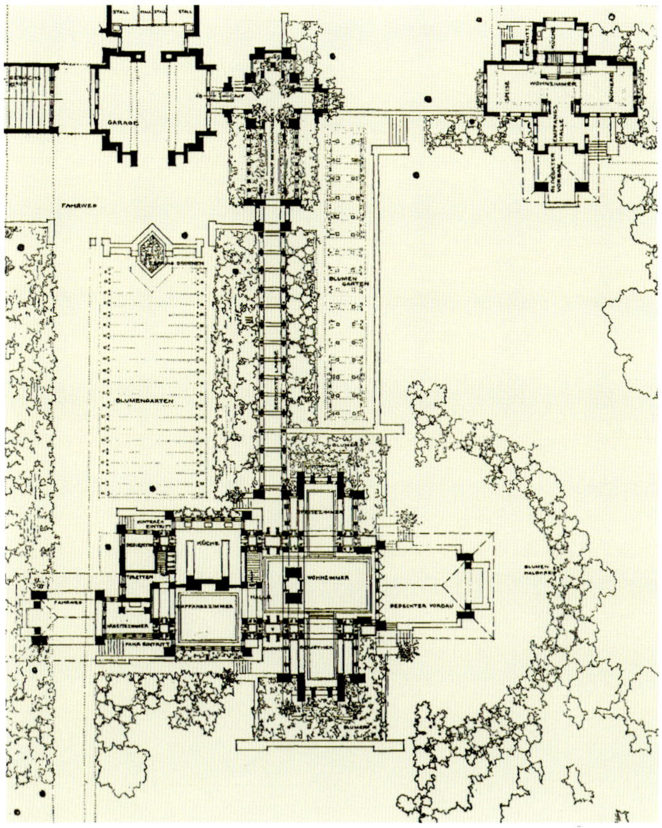

From Frank Lloyd Wright's *Ausgeführte Bauten* (originally published 1911). Photo: With kind permission of Wasmuth & Zohlen Verlag, Berlin

Fig. 7. Darwin Martin House, Buffalo, New York, by Frank Lloyd Wright, 1904. Overall site plan.

Paris in 1893 (this latter a trip with his decorator George Healy that he seems not to have mentioned afterward but is clearly documented in New York customs records). In both cases, he read his audience a poem of his own authorship and, in the case of Paris—surviving to this day in his own handwriting—in French.

These were important moments. I have wondered for years why Sullivan judged poetry to be the language to "speak" under these uniquely formal circumstances. At the end of his career, he produced two similarly puzzlingly perverse productions—masterpieces really—both also indirect. The first is his *Autobiography*, which is the account of his childhood and training down to the moment that he emerged as a leading Chicago architect with the Auditorium Building of 1886–90, but stopping just short of that greater story of the Wainwright Building (1889–90) to the Carson Pirie Scott Store (1898–1903). The second is his *System of Architectural Ornament* (1924), which after the first nine drawn folio pages explaining the elaboration of abstract ornamental patterns transforms into eleven pages of amazing functionless geometric fantasies (see fig. 8). If Sullivan rejects the Ecole method as abstract, methodical, and local, we must ask why he nonetheless praises his Paris mathematics tutor Clopet for his declaration, "Here our demonstrations shall be so broad as to admit of NO EXCEPTIONS."[12]

I suspect now, after many years of puzzlement, that this is obvious: for Sullivan, the moment suggests its "language" just as the nature of a skyscraper— "a tall and soaring thing"—suggests its architectural treatment. We should listen to him when he tells us a skyscraper is above all "a tall and soaring thing." So also, to stand and speak before the public for the first time—in English, then in French—is to use words as your "art." To end your life is to remember its beginning; to discourse on ornament is to engender it in all its wondrous fantasy.

The reason why I pose this fundamental and puzzling question is that, finally, thinking in such terms was in the end what the Beaux-Arts method was about. Instead of extending it forward, as most architects did in explaining and exercising it in actual designs like Flagg's library project, Sullivan was folding it back on its basic idea, its universality. Sullivan has freed it from abstraction and method by taking it metaphorically—and before his mind a much richer world of media and effects appeared. Most of Sullivan's East Coast contemporaries took the Beaux-Arts method literally and did not get beyond the technique of the plan. Sullivan, instead, saw it as a broad principle of expression.

Sullivan was folding [the Beaux-Arts method] back on its basic idea, its universality.

Did Frank Lloyd Wright, as Sullivan's self-proclaimed student, come to understand this in his mature, post–1900 work, and does it help us grasp his work as "Beaux-Arts"? One may immediately respond to this by emphasizing the evocative qualities of the Beaux-Arts in his presentation drawings—that it is a matter of rendering rather than architecture. Yet in certain instances, the tricks of circulation and poché seem to appear, not in his Chicago houses, but abstracted, in Wright's work itself, specifically in his plan for the Darwin Martin House in Buffalo of 1904 (fig. 7), which Edgar Tafel says Wright especially liked as a sheet and pinned it to his wall (as Louis Kahn later did with Piranesi's Campus Martius). In a sense, the public spaces of this plan are merely an elaboration of his *Ladies' Home Journal* "Prairie" type of 1901: a T-shaped

. . . Wright has taken the Paris graphic vocabulary a step further and lightened it . . .

living room-dining room-library extending out on axis and cross axis to the right, and an entry block mirroring it to the left divided down its length between kitchen and vestibule. But two important novelties appear here transforming it more overtly into a Beaux-Arts composition: Wright's two halves are thrust apart by his opening a central void which becomes the origin of an unexpected cross axis shooting out across the back property as an arbor. And, just as Wright's conventional domestic apartments step aside to permit this grand new element of circulation, that most fundamental mark of Beaux-Arts planning, poché, appears in the unique "pier clusters" pushing in on that central space at its four diagonals, these reappearing left and right to stake out and unify the entry and living room-dining room masses. Yet this is in no way overt: the pier clusters are decorative passages of larger and smaller ink squares and repeat the house's geometry as a whole. And as these scale down the spatial pattern of the house, a great arc of exterior planting scales it up responding to that geometric pattern in another scale and shape. The pattern of the house plan itself is merely a modulation between these two, the pier smaller, the flowerbed larger. Wright has taken the Paris graphic vocabulary a step further and lightened it, paralleling this abstraction but less impressionistically and more effectively.

The perspectives in Wright's *Ausgeführte Bauten* are not what is important, it is the plans—as Otto Antonia Graf's four thick volumes of analysis make clear (following earlier such analyses, especially that of Heinrich de Fries, published in 1926).[13] And there is a peculiarity of the original publication of the *Ausgeführte*

Photo: The Art Institute of Chicago/Art Resource, NY

Fig. 8. From *System of Architectural Ornament* by Louis Sullivan, 1923, plate 20, "Finis."

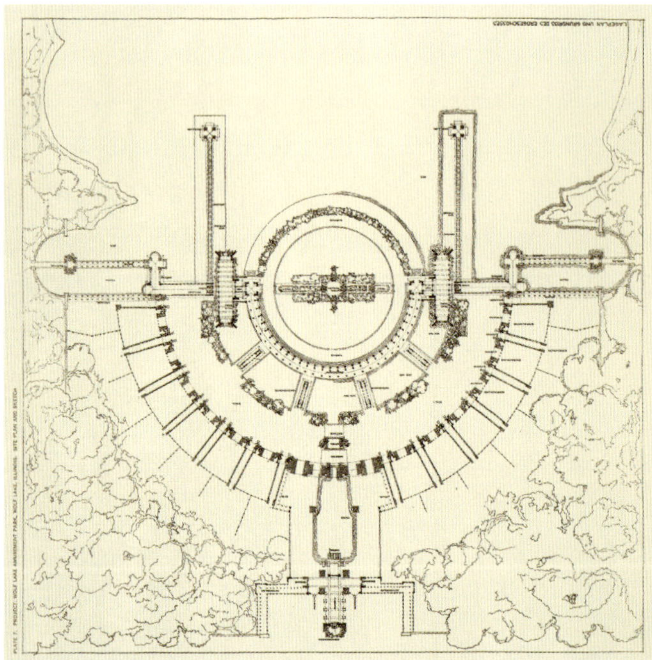

Photo: With kind permission of Wasmuth & Zohlen Verlag, Berlin

Fig. 9. Wolf Lake Amusement Park, Indiana, by Frank Lloyd Wright, 1895. Plan, reproduced in Wright's *Ausgeführte Bauten* (1911). Architect Robert Spencer wrote about Wright's work, "[I]n all his ornament there is evidence of wise and thoughtful planning, of the same synthetic method which successfully develops the ground plan of a great building." (*Architectural Review*, June 1900)

Fig. 10. Wolf Lake Amusement Park. Perspective, reproduced in Wright's *Ausgeführte Bauten* (1911).

Bauten that makes this unmistakable: unlike the many subsequent inexpensive reprintings, in the original, plans and perspectives of houses are paired pages, a board perspective and a tracing paper plan glued along its longer top edge. That is to say, Wright repeatedly obliges the reader to start with the house's plan—although with an intriguing hint of a picture to come visible literally *through* it—then revealed after carefully lifting up the delicate cover sheet. There is no way that the reader can miss his point, that the plan comes first and is the generator—literally, in the gesture of lifting the transparent page—and the actual building something only to be discovered beyond it. We have noted the complaint about Beaux-Arts work as privileging the plan over the elevation and section. Here Wright offers a response, both in how one encounters his project and in how the building actually works: the two are "transparent" to each other conceptually and literally in the lifting of those transparent cover sheets. Wright's work is "Beaux-Arts" in the very profound sense that he solves the great dilemma French planning raised, the valuing of the plan pattern at the expense of the *coup d'oeil* of the building. Perhaps this is what happens if one treats the specific medium of domestic architecture as fundamentally as Sullivan did the whole range of media comprising expression. Was it in this sense that Sullivan had moved Wright beyond what might be accomplished by a visit to the Ecole des Beaux-Arts?

We might also note that Wright devotes the next-to-last four-plate fascicle of the second volume of his *Ausgeführte Bauten* to the Coonley House of 1907 (plates LVI–LX), followed by his unbuilt McCormick mansion of circa 1908, and finally his spreading Wolf Lake amusement park of 1895 (figs. 9, 10). This is clearly not a chronological arrangement of these projects, but they are the most formal, splendid, and "Beaux-Arts" compositions of Wright's "Prairie" years. It is truly amazing to encounter these next-to-last plates in the folio. They start with the spreading Coonley House plan, in the Chicago suburb of Riverside, printed on transparent film that you have to lift to discover an aerial view taken from across the basin (a view balanced by the abstract window and plaster patterns), continuing with the McCormick plan, for a house in Lake Forest, Illinois, again transparent and glued along the top of the famous aerial view of the house seen from Lake Michigan. This then morphs to a second view of the McCormick complex seen from inland and then (this panel alone in the fascicle is without a film overlay) to the layout of the Wolf Lake, Indiana, complex of fifteen years before. This last is the most thunderous of all these compositions, which—in order to grasp in aerial view underneath—requires a unique final step of folding out the board of plate LX (see fig. 10) across the table in front of you. These are Wright's grandest plans and he presents them here, just before the end of his collection, as a kind of Beaux-Arts crescendo. A person finds him- or herself transforming the examination of this book into a labor of progressively lifting and unfolding pages as Wright must also have intended his buildings in actual encounter to have unfolded themselves spatially as the visitor walked forward.

So, to Colin Rowe's saying that Wright circa 1895 was already past what he might learn at the Ecole des Beaux-Arts itself, I would respond that Wright insinuates the signs of exactly that message very cleverly in his self-presentation in the *Ausgeführte Bauten*—enabled by the sense of geometric continuity implicit in Beaux-Arts composition, but rarely developed as a thing-in-itself as we see in Wright's plans spread out in transparent cover sheets intimating their elevations and perspectives underneath.

David Van Zanten is professor emeritus at Northwestern University, working on design methods and the architect's social sense of him- or herself. He contributed to the exhibition *The Architecture of the Ecole des Beaux-Arts* (The Museum of Modern Art, New York, 1975; catalogue edited by Arthur Drexler, 1977). He expanded on his Paris work in his books *Designing Paris* (MIT Press, 1987; awarded the Society of Architectural Historians' Hitchcock Prize, 1988) and *Building Paris* (Cambridge University Press, 1994). His parallel work on Chicago is summarized in his *Sullivan's City* (W. W. Norton, 2000) and several books about Walter Burley Griffin and Griffin's wife, the architect Marion Mahony.

Notes

1. "Ich weiss nicht ob Sullivan in Paris studiert hat, aber Wright ist ein Schüler der Ecole des Beaux-Arts." H. P. Berlage, "Neuere amerikanische Architektur," *Schweizerische Bauzeitung* 60, no. 11 (September 14, 1912): 150. Compare this to Henry-Russell Hitchcock's 1944 essay "Frank Lloyd Wright and the 'Academic Tradition' of the Early Eighteen-Nineties," *Journal of the Warburg and Courtauld Institutes* 7 (1944), 46–63.

2. Paul Turner, "Frank Lloyd Wright and the Young Le Corbusier," *Journal of the Society of Architectural Historians*, 42, no. 4 (December 1983): 350–59: "On sentait dans les plans de Wright la bonne école de l'Ecole des Beaux-arts d'ici, c'est-à-dire, un inclination vers l'ordre, vers l'organisation, vers une caractère de pure architecture."

3. Frank Lloyd Wright, *An Autobiography*, 1st ed. (New York: Longman's, Green and Co., 1932), 123–25; 2nd ed. (New York: Duell, Sloan and Pearce, 1943), 125–27. The offer, Wright says, was four years in Paris, two years in Rome.

4. There is an extensive recent literature of the Ecole doctrine and architectural composition, including Arthur Drexler, ed., *The Architecture of the Ecole des Beaux-Arts* (Cambridge, MA: MIT Press, 1977); Richard A. Etlin, *Symbolic Space: French Enlightenment Architecture and Its Legacy* (Chicago: University of Chicago Press, 1994); and Jacques Lucan, *Composition, non-composition: Architecture et théories, XIXe–XXe siècles* (Lausanne: Presses Polytechniques et Universitaires Romandes, 2009).

5. The competition specifications at the turn of the century are laid out in Henry Guédy, *L'enseignement à l'Ecole Nationale et Spéciale des Beaux-Arts, Section d'architecture* (Paris: Aulanier, n. d.), 391–432.

6. ... marchant de l'ensemble aux sous-ensembles, du corps de bâtiment à ses détails, vous avancez facilement, si votre point de départ est judicieux ..." *Eléments et théorie de l'architecture* (Paris: n. p. [1901]), vol. 1, 101.

7. Edouard Arnaud, *Cours d'architecture et de constructions civiles* (Paris: Imprimerie des Arts et Manufactures, 1928), 56: "Le travail de l'esprit y est comparable à celui que l'on fait dans la récherche d'une problème d'échec. Dans l'un et l'autre cas, il faut trouver une solution basée, non sur des principes absolus ... mais sur des combinaisons que l'imagination, aidée par une bonne méthode de travail, doit suggérer."

8. I owe my warmest thanks to Pamela Casey at Avery Drawings and Archives for her help with the Wright drawings in this and other cases.

9. Ernest Flagg, "The Proposed Tilden Trust Library," *Architectural Review* (Boston), 1, no. 8 (September 12, 1892): 69–72; see Mardges Bacon, *Ernest Flagg, Beaux-Arts Architect and Urban Reformer* (New York: Architectural History Foundation, 1986), esp. 67–68.

10. Cret's library building was immediately recognized as a model of Beaux-Arts composition—a model the architect himself explained when asked to write the entry on "library architecture" for the twelfth edition of *Encyclopedia Britannica* shortly afterward. Among Cret's writings on composition are "The Ecole des Beaux-Arts: What its Architectural Teaching Means," *Architectural Record* 23 (1908): 367–71; and "Design," in *Book of the School: Department of Architecture 1874–1934* (Philadelphia: University of Pennsylvania Press, 1934), 27–31.

11. Louis Sullivan, *The Autobiography of an Idea* (New York: Dover Publications, 1956), 240. According to the *Autobiography*, Sullivan stayed at the Ecole two years, but New York customs records show only 1874–75. Did he perhaps go back, leaving from a port other than New York?

12. We forget to ask exactly who Clopet was although the Ecole records tells us he was an architect (not a mathematician at all) and instructor at the Ecole des Arts Décoratifs (and later dismissed for some grievous and unnamed misconduct).

13. There an immense and fascinating literature of formal analysis of Wright's compositional techniques, whether focusing on Wright himself, as in Neil Levine's books (*The Architecture of Frank Lloyd Wright*, 1996, and *The Urbanism of Frank Lloyd Wright*, 2016, both published by Princeton University Press) or on his contribution to the larger question of geometric design, as in Otto Antonia Graf's *Erräumen: Zum Werk von Frank Lloyd Wright* (4 vols., Vienna: Böhlau, 2002), or on the many contributions anthologized, as in Robert McCarter's *On and by Frank Lloyd Wright: A Primer of Architectural Principles* (London: Phaidon, 2005). See also Heinrich de Fries, ed., Frank Lloyd Wright: *Aus dem Lebenswerke eines Architekten* (Berlin: Ernst Pollak, 1926).

FRANK LLOYD WRIGHT AND THE CLASSICAL PLAN

STUART COHEN

Wright flirted with classicism in the 1892 Blossom House and Milwaukee Public Library competition plans. His classically symmetrical plans in the early 1900s for Unity Temple in Oak Park, Illinois; the Larkin Building in Buffalo, New York; Midway Gardens in Chicago; and the Imperial Hotel in Tokyo, with their planning grids, central axis, and the repetition and pairing of elements, clearly show the influence of Beaux-Arts ideas.

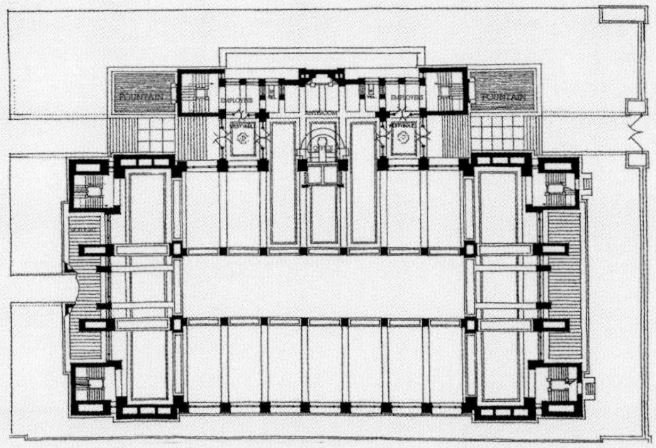

Larkin Building, Buffalo, New York, 1903

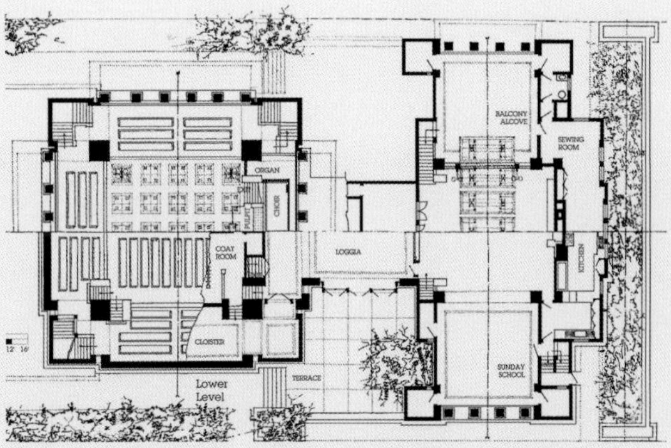

Unity Temple, Oak Park, Illinois, 1904

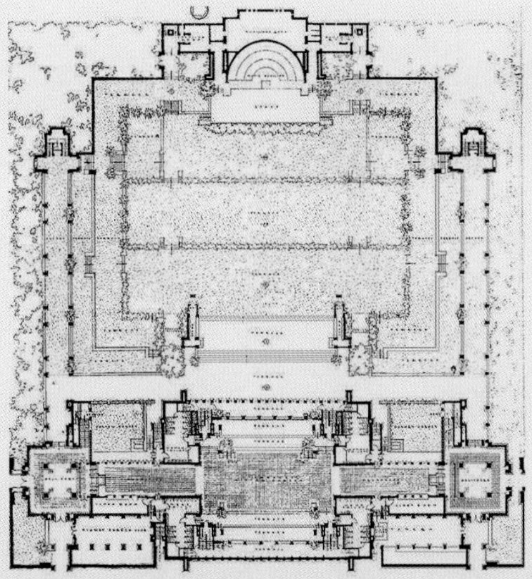

Midway Gardens, Chicago, Illinois, 1913

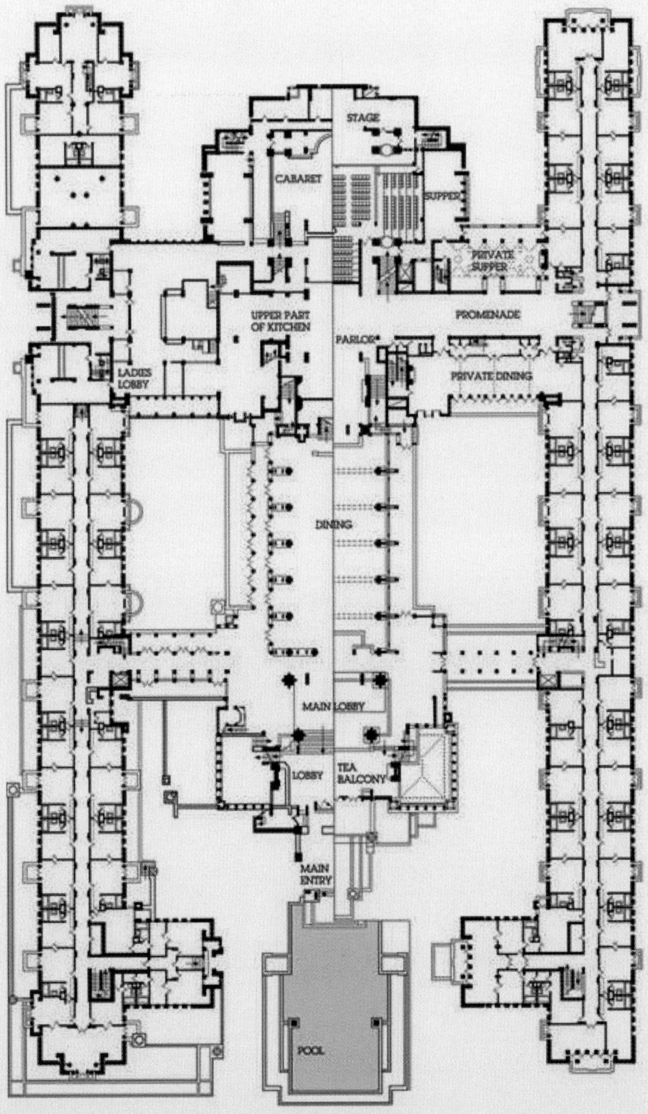

Imperial Hotel, Tokyo, Japan, 1915

CHICAGO BOARD OF TRADE
MONEY MUSEUM
SEE A MILLION DOLLARS!

CHICAGO'S SKYSCRAPER URBANISM

STUART COHEN

Today's interest in traditional urbanism, the idea that a building should be shaped by its physical context, and an interest in classicism as idealized form all seem to be at odds with the contemporary development of American cities. The construction of tall buildings in the 1960s and '70s was driven by images of "the city in the park" and zoning bonuses for open plazas along the street. It is now driven by structural engineering in the service of form making. This has failed to produce a satisfactory, let alone humane, version of the public domain. These buildings totally disregard the potential of the skyscraper to engage with the city street or respond to issues of urban context.

The skyscrapers of the 1920s and '30s seemed to understand this potential. Perhaps this is what was being suggested by Werner Hegemann and Elbert Peets when they wrote, in their 1922 compendium of great urban spaces, *The American Vitruvius: An Architects' Handbook of Civic Art,* "The intelligent use of the skyscraper in civic design will be America's most valuable contribution to civic art."[1]

How are we to reconcile this prediction with the late twentieth-century development of the skyscraper? For America's tall buildings of the 1920s and '30s, this was not an issue. Zoning and building codes required setbacks to ensure light and air at the street. The schema was to fill out the site at its base. This provided definition of the street. Skyscrapers then tapered or set back into a tower to present a profiled, often romantic silhouette when seen from a distance. Thus, these buildings with a nonfigural lower mass could act as a "ground" to the adjacent street space. The idea that a tall building could simultaneously be both a figure (foreground) and a ground (background) can be seen in building ensembles such as the relationship of the Church of Sant'Agnese in Rome to the other buildings encircling the Piazza Navona.[2] The church's dome and towers establish a presence in the space while the church's facade remains part of the defining wall of the plaza.

Fig. 1. Chicago Board of Trade Building, designed by Holabird & Root, 1929–30.

If we consider the layout of most traditional cities, including grid cities, it is easy to understand the potential of skyscrapers to be used urbanistically.

The skyscraper . . . will be America's most valuable contribution to civic art.

They can act as urban gateposts marking important points of transition in a city, terminate a vista, create a focus within a space, and even define an urban space. Chicago was where the skyscraper originated, and the city features many examples of skyscraper urbanism.

As a city laid out on a grid, Chicago offers few opportunities for terminating streets with a building. An important exception is the Board of Trade Building, part of a unique building ensemble at the end of La Salle Street, the center of Chicago's financial district. As early as 1885, the street ended in the facade of the "old" Board of Trade Building designed by William W. Boyington, the architect of Chicago's "Gothic-style" Water Tower and Pumping Station on North Michigan Avenue. La Salle Street was visually terminated by the Board of Trade's clock tower that rose 300 feet above the pavement. On either side of the foot of the street, facing each other, are the Federal Reserve Bank of 1922 whose articulated base was built at the scale of the main block of Boyington's building, and to the west,

From *The Architectural Work of Graham, Anderson, Probst and White, Chicago* (London, B. T. Batsford, 1933)

Fig. 2. Proposal for a new building by Graham, Anderson, Probst & White for the Board of Trade with portico entries to match the adjacent bank buildings. Undated drawing, probably mid-1920s.

the Continental Illinois Bank, built in 1924. Both were designed by Graham, Anderson, Probst & White, the successor firm to D. H. Burnham & Company. These buildings each feature two-story classical entry porticos, which push the main facades back from the street, and along with the Board of Trade, create a shallow symmetrical space. The pairing and the scale of the porticos establish a cross axis that further reinforces the perception that La Salle Street ends in an urban space rather than a building facade (fig. 1). It was in response to this defined urban space that Graham, Anderson, Probst & White put forward a proposal (unbuilt) for the Board of Trade that would have terminated the street in a third two-story portico (fig. 2). The current Board of Trade Building, constructed in 1929–30, was designed by Holabird & Root. The development of its massing reinforces its function as a terminus to La Salle Street. It is clearly based on Bertram Goodhue's unbuilt entry for the 1922 Chicago Tribune Tower Competition. The Board of Trade has similar massing and window treatment. Goodhue's Tribune Tower design ended in a pyramidal top to be crowned by a statue of Mercury, the messenger of the gods. The Board of Trade is similarly capped by a pyramid, but here it is surmounted by a statue of Ceres, goddess of the harvest. The tapering shaft of Goodhue's design sets back by dropping off its corners to articulate the ascending central mass into a cruciform-shaped point tower. The Holabird & Root design provides a base that defines the street at street level, with a clock as a centralized element. The building then sets back in steps at its center, reversing the Goodhue design and suggesting an apse-like recess that functions to receive the axis of the street at the scale of the city. This spatial complex is an urban ensemble formed entirely of skyscrapers that evolved as a series of responses to a unique location in the city.

... La Salle Street ends in an urban space rather than a building facade.

The creation of a large-scale urban space at a significant location in the city may be seen in the sequential development of the space around the Michigan Avenue Bridge. Here the Chicago Tribune Tower and its surrounding structures—the Wrigley Building, the London Guaranty and Accident Company Building (later named the Stone Container Building), and 333 North Michigan Avenue—form an extraordinary grouping of skyscrapers, built independently over time, that work to define an urban space as a gateway to the north (figs. 3, 4).

Originally there was no bridge connecting South Michigan Avenue (then called Michigan Boulevard) and Pine Street, which was to the north of the Chicago River. Before their Michigan Boulevard plan of 1909, Daniel Burnham and Edward Bennett proposed the construction of a plaza that would span the river. This included a classical building terminating the northern axis of Michigan Avenue, formally resolving the misalignment of Michigan Avenue and Pine Street behind it. The plaza would have served as a significant point of transition in

Photo: © Tom Rossiter Photography. Courtesy of Goettsch Partners, restoration architect for 333 North Michigan Avenue, the London Guaranty and Accident Company Building (London House), and the Wrigley Building.

Fig. 3. Michigan Avenue Bridge looking south, showing (left to right) the Illinois Center, 333 North Michigan Avenue, the London Guaranty and Accident Company Building, and the Wrigley Building.

Photo: Justin Prenton

Fig. 4. Michigan Avenue Bridge looking north, showing the Wrigley Building (left) and Chicago Tribune Tower (right).

From American Architect, December 11, 1918

Fig. 5. Proposal for North Michigan Avenue by Andrew Rebori, 1918.

From American Architect, December 11, 1918

Fig. 6. Proposal for North Michigan Avenue by Andrew Rebori, 1918

the city. In 1910, Benjamin Marshall proposed spanning the river not with a bridge, but with a giant triumphal arch that the street would run through.[3]

In 1912, property owners north of the river formed the North Central Business District Association. They commissioned a number of Chicago architects, including Andrew Rebori and Howard Van Doren Shaw, to propose plans for the extension of North Michigan Avenue. Recognition of the importance of the bridge and the development of North Michigan Avenue, as a major link between the two sides of the river, is delineated in early proposals made by Rebori. He published several designs for the area at the bridge and for the imagined extension of Michigan Avenue north of the river. In the first he proposed two paired office towers joined by a triumphal arch (fig. 5), perhaps influenced by Marshall's design.

In his next proposal, Rebori included a space of arrival between two splayed seven-story buildings with a pair of office towers, as gateposts, at the north end of the space (fig. 6). These are shown flanking the entrance to the street. The space also takes up the axial shift between the street to the north and the street to the south of the Chicago River. In Rebori's third proposal, titled, "Chicago Practical," made in 1915 and published in *American Architect* in 1918, Rebori proposed two rounded "Gothic-style" towers, again, large-scale gateposts, emphasizing their function as points in space by making them onmidirectional. Their national publication and the overall massing of these towers suggest that they could have had an influence on Howells & Hood's winning entry in the Tribune Tower Competition (figs. 7, 8).

The Wrigley Building was the first building of this urban ensemble to be constructed. William Wrigley Jr., the chewing gum magnate, purchased the site for his building in 1918, knowing that eventually a bridge would be constructed at this location, although it was not completed until 1921. In 1919, Wrigley commissioned Graham, Anderson, Probst & White to design his building. A partner in the firm, Peirce Anderson, designed a white terra-cotta clad office block with its angled face splayed to follow the angle of the Chicago River to the west. At the center of Anderson's facade was a central

From *American Architect*, December 11, 1918

Fig. 7. Proposal for North Michigan Avenue, rendering by Andrew Rebori, 1918.

From *Chicago Architects* (Chicago: Swallow Press, 1976), 67

Fig 8. Aerial view of North Michigan Avenue, c. 1970.

tower patterned after the Giralda Tower of the Seville Cathedral. The Wrigley Building was fully rented when it opened in 1920, and in 1923 Wrigley constructed an annex building to the north. It was identical in finish and detail to the original and was connected at the ground level by a two-story arcade screen that ties the two buildings together. The completion of the bridge was shown in a perspective drawing that includes the "bridge houses" designed by Edward Bennett (fig. 9). The drawing announces that their construction marks a "first step in making this gateway as famous as the Place de la Concorde in Paris." It also features the completed Wrigley Building, and, across the river, a continuous wall of buildings along South Water Street—a placeholder that turns from South Water Street (now Wacker Drive) onto Michigan Avenue and cups back in an exedra shape at the corner to define a shallow space at the north side of the bridge. This is the corner strategy that Alfred Alschuler would use in his 1922–23 design for the classical London Guaranty and Accident Company Building, a curved front office tower topped by a colonnade of Corinthian columns and a circular lantern.

In 1922, the Chicago Tribune company planned to build an office tower for its own use along North Michigan Avenue immediately in front of the newspaper's printing plant, which was completed in 1921 and designed by Jarvis Hunt. The Tribune had purchased the land in 1919 while the bridge was under construction. An international competition for the tower was announced on June 10, 1922, asking for "the design of the most beautiful office building in the world."

The Tribune Tower competition drew hundreds of entries from all over the world. The winner was a "Gothic-style" tower design by Howells & Hood of New York, based on the south tower of Rouen Cathedral. The architects understood that their building would stand at the edge of an urban space forming a gatepost and situated so that it would dominate the view looking east from the river and South Water Street. They wrote, "The structure is carried to its full height as a square on the Michigan Avenue front only, thus always giving the same impression from where ever and showing the same from all points as the Tribune's landmark."[4]

From *American Architect*, May 11, 1921.

Fig. 9. "New Gateway of the Greater Chicago." View of Michigan Avenue Bridge looking south.

The competition designs, shown in perspectives, were published by the Tribune company in a book documenting the competition. The most influential were those by Eliel Saarinen and Bertram Goodhue. The Saarinen design, lauded by Louis Sullivan, would influence the form of a generation of skyscrapers in the 1930s. Without a clear termination, the repetitive windows, and the building's setbacks, suggested the structure's continued vertical extension. For Sullivan, it was the ultimate solution to his dictum that a skyscraper should be lofty. The most iconic and surely least understood entry, however, was that of Adolf Loos, who proposed a skyscraper in the form of a giant Doric column. Putting aside the symbolism of the column, or suggested verbal puns such as "newspaper column," the building's design only makes sense as a recognition of the significance of the site (fig. 10). Loos was one of the few European entrants who had been to Chicago and would have understood that the site was a gateway to the north. Further, Loos's writings make clear that he only objected to the use of ornament on utilitarian structures, not on civic buildings. At the time of the competition, Loos was living in Paris and the resemblance to Claude-Nicolas Ledoux's design for gates at the Place de la Nation is unmistakable, making his Tribune Tower design both an idealized classical reference and a site-specific proposal. (fig. 11)

The final element of the building's ensemble was constructed at the southeast corner of Michigan Avenue and South Water Street in 1927–28. Designed by Holabird & Root, the building is known only by its address, 333 North Michigan Avenue. The architects chose to vertically articulate the north end of the building with the building's main bulk extending south along the street. The building's south end is articulated as a narrow vertical tower, which, according to John Holabird, was influenced by Eliel Saarinen's entry in the Tribune Tower competition. What is most remarkable about the north end of the building is the way it presents as a narrow point tower directly on axis with the center of Michigan Avenue, a result of the angled shift in alignment of the street that begins at the bridge.[5]

Although this grouping of buildings lacks spatial enclosure, it does define an urban space. Quintessentially American, it is a space of transition rather than repose, and one of America's most important urban spaces defined entirely by skyscrapers. While, the same may be said for Rockefeller Center in New York, built somewhat later, the architects of Rockefeller Center shared a commission that ensured the unity of the project, while in Chicago, the architects who built at the Michigan Avenue Bridge shared only an idea.

Photo: Courtesy of Thomas Kemmer

Fig. 10. Adolf Loos's entry in the Chicago Tribune Tower Competition, as it might look today on the site had it been built. Contemporary visualization and reconstruction by Thomas Kemmer.

From *Claude-Nicolas Ledoux: 1736–1806* by Michel Gallet (Paris: Picard, 1980)

Fig. 11. Gates at the Place de la Nation, Paris, by Claude-Nicolas Ledoux.

This idea, the city composed of defined public space, was seen by them as compatible with the scale of the American city and with the skyscraper. Today, at a time when skyscrapers are being given a variety of twisting, gyrating, and cantilevered forms, the idea of a vertically differentiated tower using the specifics of its form to respond to its urban site, seems a rational and eminently arguable starting point for a skyscraper's design.

Stuart Cohen is a practicing architect with a distinguished residential practice whose work is frequently published in shelter magazines. He is a Fellow of the American Institute of Architects, and the recipient of the ICAA's 2018 Arthur Ross Award for his writings. Cohen is the author of four books on Chicago's historic architecture and is Professor of Architecture Emeritus at the University of Illinois at Chicago, where he taught architectural design. He has been a visiting critic and lecturer at universities throughout the United States, including Harvard and the University of Notre Dame.

Notes

This article is based on previous articles by the author. See "The Tall Building Urbanistically Reconsidered," *Threshold: Journal of the School of Architecture University of Illinois at Chicago* (New York: Rizzoli, 1993), 12–15; and "Loos Speculation," in *The Chicago Architectural Journal*, vol. 3 (New York, Rizzoli, 1983), 1215.

1. Werner Hegemann and Elbert Peets, *The American Vitruvius: An Architects' Handbook of Civic Art* (New York: The Architectural Book Publishing Co., 1922), 147.

2. Colin Rowe and Fred Koetter propose this reading of the Church of Sant'Agnese in their book *Collage City* (Cambridge, MA: MIT Press, 1978), 77.

3. Illustrated in John Zukowsky and Jean Guarino, *Benjamin H. Marshall: Chicago Architect* (New York: Acanthus Press, with the Benjamin Marshall Society, 2015), 149.

4. *The International Competition for a New Administration Building for the Chicago Tribune: Containing All the Designs Submitted in Response to The Chicago Tribune's $1000,000 Offer Commemorating its Seventy Fifth Anniversary June 10, 1922* (Chicago: The Tribune Co., 1923). Reprinted in full in *Late Entries to The Chicago Tribune Tower Competition*, by Stanley Tigerman, introduction by Stuart Cohen, 2 vols. (New York: Rizzoli, 1981), documenting an exhibition of the same name curated by Tigerman and Cohen.

5. Because of the angle of the street, the old Water Tower sits on the central axis of Michigan Avenue looking north from the bridge.

MODERN CLASSICISM IN CHICAGO, 1970–1990s

EDWARD KEEGAN

The death of German-born Ludwig Mies van der Rohe on August 17, 1969, was the most consequential inflection point in Chicago's architecture since the 1893 opening of the World's Columbian Exposition. While the latter spawned the City Beautiful movement, which brought classical art, architecture, and urban design to almost every settled region of the United States (as well as the country's extensive international territories), Mies's passing—although internationally notable—was more local in its direct effects. Mies had arrived in Chicago in 1937 to take over the architecture program at the Armour Institute, soon rebranded as the Illinois Institute of Technology (IIT) with a Mies-designed campus. In the final three-plus decades of his life, he came to dominate the city's approach to architecture, and ultimately define the very essence of Chicago's architectural culture, including how its earlier work was commonly framed and understood.

Mies's death created an opening for a serious reappraisal and reevaluation of Chicago's architectural production.

Mies's influence on the city could seem downright hysterical. Chicago architect Ben Weese once confessed that he had attended Mies's seventy-fifth birthday party at the Arts Club: "[That] was the closest I ever got to him because I purposely never wanted to meet him," he recalled. "I thought I might get infected." But such hysteria actually had a precedent in Chicago: the vitriolic reaction of Louis Sullivan and Frank Lloyd Wright to Daniel Burnham's classical turn at the World's Fair continued to inform much of the Chicago architectural community's reaction to classical and traditional work throughout the twentieth century.

In the mid-twentieth century, Mies's acolytes portrayed the city's architecture as a linear development of "modern" forms and space that disallowed alternate histories or practices. Historians Sigfried Giedion and Carl Condit penned distinctly constrained views of Chicago's architectural legacy, which placed structural and engineering problem-solving as the primary source of aesthetic and cultural outcomes.

But Mies's death—and the obviously inferior nature of much work produced by his successors—created an opening for a serious reappraisal and reevaluation of the city's architectural production during the 1970s and '80s. A small group of like-driven local architects, all born in the 1930s or early '40s, tied together through mutual though fluctuating friendships, coalesced during the late 1960s and early '70s, and eventually changed the landscape of the city's architectural community over the next two decades.

Stanley Tigerman (1930–2019) was the self-styled "instigator." One of the oldest of this new generation, he had put up his shingle in 1962. Laurence (Larry) Booth (b. 1936) and James Nagle (b. 1937) worked for Tigerman from 1965 to 1966 before leaving to start their own small firm, which existed until 1980, when they split into separate offices. Thomas Beeby (b. 1941) and Stuart Cohen (b. 1942) recall visiting Tigerman shortly after finishing their studies and moving back to Chicago. Beeby worked for the large C. F. Murphy firm from 1965 to 1971, before joining James Hammond as a partner in 1971. Cohen opened an office in 1972 after working for several firms in New York. And Ben Weese (b. 1929) worked with

Fig. 1. Thomas Beeby, Harold Washington Library Center, Chicago, designed 1988.

Photo: Judith Bromley, courtesy of HBRA Architects

his brother Harry's large firm for two decades before leaving in 1977 to start his own small shop.

Nagle recalls that the group was frustrated by the city's architectural scene. "Seventy-four was a recession time," he says. "We had time to look around and wonder, why isn't the world more interesting and better? And there were these other people who had practiced in the city during similar hard times."

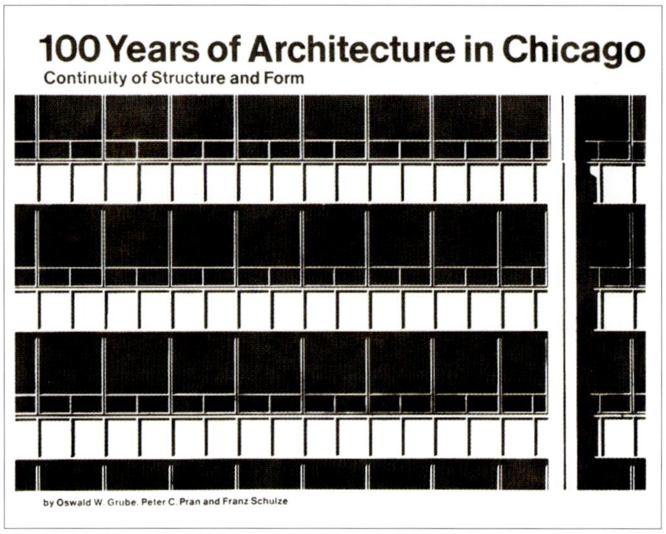

Fig. 2. Catalogue from the exhibition *100 Years of Architecture in Chicago: Continuity of Structure and Form,* 1976.

The group eventually found a voice in 1976, when Tigerman and Cohen co-curated an exhibition called *Chicago Architects* as a counterpoint to *100 Years of Architecture in Chicago: Continuity of Structure and Form*—an exhibition of the prevailing orthodox modernist view of the city's architecture first presented in Europe in 1973, and subsequently updated for an exhibition at Chicago's Museum of Contemporary Art in 1976. Tigerman would refer to *Chicago Architects* as a *salon de refusés.*

Viewing the competing catalogues for the two exhibitions side by side today is instructive (figs. 2, 3). Once, they appeared to be almost diametrically opposed; now, not so much. *Chicago Architects* was about revealing the diversity of the city's legacy beyond the Giedion-Condit-constricted structuralist story told by their Miesian rivals. And yet the more "diverse" collection of buildings—while selected to avoid the strict constructionist slant of the predominant history of Chicago then in vogue—moved the needle just a little bit. Although there's a dab of Howard Van Doren Shaw, Benjamin Marshall, and David Adler, it's hardly enough to acknowledge the lush early twentieth-century classically inspired production that still dots Chicago's North Shore and Gold Coast. But upon the exhibition's opening in March 1976 at the Cooper Union in New York, Ada Louis Huxtable in the *New York Times* called both the show and Cohen's catalogue essay "revisionist history." "The show is an iconographic feast and an exercise in provocative scholarship," she wrote.

Fig. 3. Catalogue from the exhibition *Chicago Architects,* 1976.

Later that year, the friends added IIT Dean James Ingo Freed (b. 1930) to their insurgency, and dubbed themselves the "Chicago Seven" after the political radicals of Chicago's 1968 Democratic National Convention. They then mounted an exhibition at Richard Gray's North Michigan Avenue gallery. Each showed a single house design, in drawings and a model, and they were all for sale. Memories vary, but it seems several drawings may have sold, although no one was willing to purchase an actual design for construction—which obviously could have been a boon to the small office workloads. While none of the seven designs fit the easy stereotype of the corporate Miesian aesthetic, only Beeby's mythology-based *The House of Virgil Built in Anticipation of the Return of the Golden Age* (fig. 4) can be seen as a precursor to a more classical or even traditional approach to architecture.

"Birds in flight, a blazing rainbow, and languorous nude maidens carry Beeby's conceptualizations far beyond orthodox renderings," *Chicago Tribune* architecture critic Paul Gapp wrote of the project. "The house becomes a joyous collection of spaces and shapes, but ultimately becomes a statement which seems to go beyond architecture." This was in sharp contrast to the other renderings, which Gapp noted, "range from mildly interesting to mundane."

The group reprised the exhibition the following year, adding Helmut Jahn for a total of eight participants, and mounted a subsequent exhibition that expanded the count to eleven with the inclusion of Jerry Horn, Ken Schroeder, and Cindy Weese. In 1978, members held a townhouse competition at the Graham Foundation, displaying winning entries from eight younger individuals, who enlarged the group that in 1979 formed the nucleus of the reconstituted Chicago Architectural Club.

In 1979, Beeby designed an addition for the North Shore Congregation Israel. His brick-clad Palladio-inspired design for the North Shore suburb of Glencoe, Illinois, was a direct rebuke to the congregation's existing building, a lyrically composed concrete sanctuary by Minoru Yamasaki. The client's brief, as recalled by Beeby, was to "meld two traditions," which were described as the "elegant, Classical Sephardic synagogues of Spain, Venice, and Amsterdam" and the "rustic, vernacular Ashkenazic synagogues of Eastern Europe." Beeby told *Architectural Record*, which published the addition in June 1983, that his building incorporated Mies, Asplund, Wright, Sullivan, and Kahn as well, noting, "Who knows where ideas come from?"

Fig. 4. Thomas Beeby, *The House of Virgil Built in Anticipation of the Return of the Golden Age*, featured in the Chicago Seven exhibition at the Richard Gray Gallery, Chicago, 1977.

The seemingly offhand comment, from one of Chicago's most thoughtful and articulate architects, can be seen as emblematic of the work of the era in general, and this particular group of Chicago architects specifically. It's not that none of them cared—they all very much did, if in somewhat uneven regard for delving into actual scholarship—but Beeby's attitude freed him to explore a diverse series of influences through an artist's rather than a scholar's lens, and equally allowed him to move forward without the stultifying straitjacket that had hampered the Miesians. The resulting intimate square sanctuary set within a circular envelope, thoughtfully decorated with details ranging from Doric columns to ram's horn-shaped railings, demonstrates a highly synthetic approach to architecture that embraces an inclusiveness toward historical form that seemed so alluring at the time.

The June 1980 edition of *Progressive Architecture* turned a spotlight on Chicago, with work of the "Seven" at the fore. But interestingly, this extensive coverage of the city's collective output, more than a decade after Mies's passing and four years after *Chicago Architects,* didn't include much that can be considered either classical or traditional. The cover featured Helmut Jahn's "Late Entry to the Chicago Tribune Tower Competition," part of an elaborate international exhibition of the same title organized by Tigerman and Cohen with gallerist Rhona Hoffman (fig. 5).

Included were Tigerman's Villa Proeh (1979–80) and Booth's Herman Miller Health Science Division Building (1979), which employ classical plans, but not forms. Nagle's South Side House incorporates an arched entry in an otherwise modern brick box. Even the work of Beeby, whose firm receives portfolio treatment, includes three frankly modern structures among five projects. But Cohen and Weese hew traditional, the former with a speculative Tudor home, the latter with a bank inspired by Louis Sullivan's work. It's clear from the entire issue of the magazine that Chicago by now had become a more eclectic place, but the role of classicism seems tepid at this time.

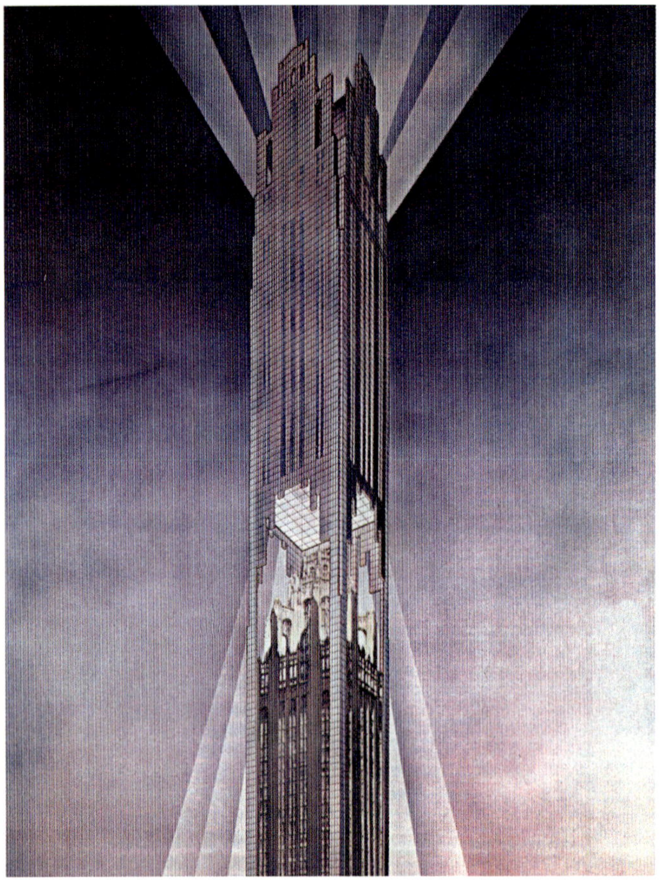

Fig. 5. Helmut Jahn, addition to the Chicago Tribune Tower, for the exhibition *Late Entries to the Chicago Tribune Tower Competition,* 1981.

Fig. 6. Laurence (Larry) Booth (Booth Hansen), House of Light, Chicago, 1983.

Booth's House of Light (1983) (fig. 6) expanded on the architect's increasing interest in traditional form. Named a Record House by *Architectural Record* in 1984, its central stair hall provided the cover for the July 1985 issue of *Architecture.* "I think we've all had our fill of funereal buildings," Booth told the *Record.* "We now want things to be light, lively, and delicate." But despite its distance from his more modern works, the house remains a highly abstracted work whose most classical elements are primarily appliqué.

The Evelyn Chapel (1984) at Illinois Wesleyan University in Bloomington, by Weese, was featured on the cover of *Architecture*'s January 1985 issue (fig. 8). Building on his seemingly perennial interest in combining vernacular and traditional vocabularies, Weese described his attempt to "bridge between historic replication and tabula rasa by modifying, combining, and permuting known and experienced shapes and forms."

Beeby's Sulzer Regional Library (designed 1980, completed 1985) built on the architect's earlier attempts to create a hybrid design of traditional and classical, melding the constructional clarity of Mies with neoclassical idioms based on Schinkel. Rooftop acroteria, scaled to the library's status as a neighborhood building, foreshadow the gargantuan motifs that top Beeby's Harold Washington Library Center at the end of the decade.

The two most clearly classical buildings designed by Tigerman are located on a single Chicago block, on Ontario Street between Dearborn and Clark. The first, a single-story-tall EIFS-clad orangery was produced as a restaurant for the then-popular Hard Rock Cafe. Completed in 1985, it was Tigerman's whimsy that drove the depiction of rock 'n roll cool using straight Tuscan (albeit stucco/Styrofoam) classicism.

Stuart Cohen's Carrigan Townhouse (1984), designed with Anders Nereim and published in *Architectural*

Digest, inserted interlocking multilevel John Soane-inspired spaces into a nineteenth-century North Side Chicago structure (fig. 7). The project definitively moved Cohen beyond theory and into actual building, drawing subsequent commissions, almost exclusively residential, that continue to the present day in his practice with his wife and partner, Julie Hacker.

The reigning design partner of Skidmore, Owings & Merrill, Bruce Graham, initially dismissed the exhibition *Chicago Architects*—not least because of its celebration of in-house rival Walter Netsch as part of the extended Chicago narrative. But even Graham would eventually surrender to the pull of history later in the decade. His protégé, Adrian Smith, would design an abstracted Richardsonian arch for Neiman Marcus (1983) on Michigan Avenue and move on to even more classically inspired work like Boston's Rowes Wharf (1987) and Chicago's NBC Building (1989). The architectural success of Rowes Wharf was immediately apparent, as it graced the March 1988 cover of *Architectural Record* (fig. 9).

In 1988, Beeby completed the Daniel F. and Ada L. Rice Building for the Art Institute of Chicago. As architecture critic Paul Goldberger pointed out in the *New York Times*, this wasn't the first "turn back" for the art museum—a renovation of its original 1893 building completed the previous year had installed traditional moldings to its earliest galleries, to designs by SOM. Beeby's addition was featured on the cover of *Progressive Architecture* that November, and Pilar Viladas noted the design's "almost perversely contemporary spin" on classicism—"the balusters, which appear in elevation as flat, Doric-column paper dolls, are in fact solid, rectangular blocks that are chamfered at the corners." This same motif would be reprised by Beeby in the cast-in-place concrete columns within the loft-like spaces of the Harold Washington Library Center.

That same year, recent University of Notre Dame alumni David Mayernik and Thomas Rajkovich, both employees of Beeby, debuted as the first wave

Photo: Nick Merrick/Hedrich-Blessing

Fig. 7. Stuart Cohen (Stuart Cohen & Anders Nereim Architects), Carrigan Townhouse, 1984.

Photo: © John R. Brzezinski, universityicons.com

Fig. 8. Ben Weese, Evelyn Chapel, Illinois Wesleyan University, Bloomington, Illinois, 1984.

of the next generation of Chicago's classical architects, producing a project for the completion of the Capitol Mall in St. Paul, Minnesota. Their unflinching embrace of precedent, uninfected with the Miesian modernism or irony of their mentors, placed Cass Gilbert's classical state capitol in a setting that would have appealed to the original architect three-quarters of a decade later.

Also in 1988, Beeby's Harold Washington Library Center won a public competition, resulting in Chicago's most traditional public building since the Great Depression (fig. 1). Its thick masonry exterior walls were set against a fourth curtain wall of glass that extended to all four sides under crowning pediments ornamented with exuberantly oversized acroteria. Remaining true to the architect's synthetic approach, it was both Beeby's most classical, and yet still so very postmodern building.

Adjacent to the earlier Hard Rock Cafe, Tigerman created his most straightforward classical design for a two-story transformer substation (completed 1989) for municipal electric power provider Commonwealth Edison (fig. 10). Security concerns for the unoccupied structure required a more substantial construction technique than usual, resulting in a brick and limestone two-story solution that gained from the reuse of carved stone decoration from the original 1929 structure on the site. But Tigerman would quickly retreat from his toe dips in the classical waters, although his wife and architectural partner, Margaret McCurry, would continue to use traditional and classical forms in her own erudite output, which would constitute much of the firm's residential work in the 1990s and early decades of the twenty-first century.

Photo: © Nick Wheeler | Wheeler Photographics compliments of SOM

Fig. 9. Adrian Smith (Skidmore, Owings & Merrill), Rowes Wharf, Boston, 1987.

As director of the school of architecture at the University of Illinois at Chicago (UIC), Tigerman brought Thomas Gordon Smith to teach at the school in 1986. At the decade's close, Smith moved one hundred miles east to South Bend, Indiana, where he created the curriculum and atmosphere for a recasting of classicism for contemporary practice at the University of Notre Dame.

Through sheer force of personality, hard work, and unparalleled networking, Tigerman dominated Chicago's post-Miesian architectural landscape. What he didn't do himself, he either encouraged others to do, or assumed credit after the fact. Tigerman, no doubt, saw himself as a Philip Johnson-styled Chicago kingmaker. Architect John Macsai summarized Tigerman's omnivorous attitude in a cartoon for the 1989 *Chicago Architectural Club Journal* that depicts Tigerman as a rooster-tailed weathervane that can point toward any of the period's trends—Mies, postmodernism, classicism, anti-functionalism, deconstructionism, not-yet-invented-ism, or modernism.

While Chicago had entered the 1970s with a more clearly defined crisis—the death of Mies—than other locales, at the conclusion of the ensuing two decades, there began a return to the city's modernist formal roots, rather than a large-scale embracing of the classical and traditional. Unlike the East Coast in general (and New York in particular), where the same period of time provided tacit approval and encouragement for several generations of practitioners to flourish with classically oriented practices, the moment in Chicago was shorter-lived. Of the seven agents provocateurs, only Beeby and his office's leadership would continue to build in a classical vein in subsequent decades. Freed returned to New York in 1978 and ceased to be an influence on the Chicago scene. Nagle never embraced any type of classical design. Tigerman and Booth quickly retreated by the early 1990s. Weese would continue to explore a more vernacular-based version of both the traditional and modern. Cohen's work would be most transformed by the period, but while always informed by the classical, would remain staunchly in the less rarefied air of the traditional.

Photo: Courtesy of The Art Institute of Chicago

Fig. 10. Stanley Tigerman (Tigerman, Fugman, McCurry), Commonwealth Edison Substation, Chicago, 1989.

Of the generation whose educations occurred during the 1970s and '80s (who often studied with or worked for members of the Seven), those most affected include Rajkovich, Mayernick, R. Michael Graham, Phillip Liederbach, and Aric Lasher. Except for Mayernick, who uses Notre Dame as his base of operations (with most of his built work in Italy), they all continue to produce classical work in Chicago. Liederbach and Graham met and studied together under Tigerman, Beeby, Booth, and Cohen at UIC, but their considerable body of work remains more traditional than classical. And Lasher, who now holds the design reins at Beeby's firm (renamed HBRA in 1999), continues to produce highly synthetic classical work that builds on Beeby's voracious approach to architectural precedent.

Now fifty years after the death of Mies—and more than a quarter century after the close of the postmodern period, it's worth asking why classicism hasn't flourished in Chicago as it has in other places. The genuine handful of practitioners in the genre—including Beeby, Cohen, Graham, Liederbach, Rajkovich, and Lasher—produce work that's every bit the equal of that being done around the country and by their Europe-based contemporaries. But the lack of a wider scene of contemporary classicists might be seen as an inevitable outgrowth of its 1970s roots. While all seven of the original Chicago protagonists seemed sincere in their attempt to widen the architectural conversation, many of them weren't interested in widening it too much. All staunch civic boosters, their investment in Chicago's "modern" legacy of architecture ultimately proved too much for most. And the small remnant, slightly increased in number by their former students and employees, finds itself as a perpetual *salon de refusés* in the architectural community.

Edward Keegan is an architect, writer, curator, broadcaster, and educator who has used these diverse platforms as an outspoken critic and strong advocate for Chicago and its unique architectural legacy for more than three decades.

A NOVELIST OF THE PAST AMONGST HISTORIANS OF THE FUTURE

ARIC LASHER

For better or for worse, I was taught that if you loved architecture, you loved it all, and if you grasped first principles, you could find in works of all kinds that which relates them to one another and allows you to love them equally. I was never taught that some ideas were forbidden, or that demonstrably good ones could grow obsolete. The depth of my loves didn't allow me to discard things that I have since been told are only acceptably appreciated at a distance, entombed in the amber of historical perspective. History could serve modernity through transformation, opposition, or extension. But it could not be ignored. Your course of practice was your own choice, but architecture was ideally an art capable of absorbing many, and often opposing, means to reach the same ends.

I am now an architect in Chicago, a city for which the grid of its streets and the frames of its buildings provide a unifying scaffold for a multitude of ideas expressed through architecture. I am also, as it were, interested in both the classicism of the grid and the fullness that recognizable, architectural expression might impart to it.

The sanctioned narrative of Chicago architecture is compelling and, as usually presented, consistent. It shows a relentless and glorious trajectory away from the subjectivities of evolved languages or inherited cultures toward a universal and neutralizing modernity. The greatest examples that buoy this narrative are breathtaking, hence its vigorous embrace by both architects and the public: Burnham & Root's Monadnock Building, Sullivan's Carson Pirie Scott Store, Mies's Lake Shore Drive Apartments and Crown Hall, C. F. Murphy's Daley Center, SOM and Smith+Gill's current supertalls, and Ronan's Poetry Foundation. Still, potent exceptions in this city betray the persistence of familiar, inherited form in the buildings of great practitioners and in the affections of its citizens. Works designed by Atwood, Adler, Rebori, and Shaw, or the pioneering corporate practices of Holabird & Roche and Graham, Anderson, Probst & White are hard to ignore but are often brushed aside as speed bumps on the road to an apotheosis of unencumbered modernism.

I was never taught that some ideas were forbidden, or that demonstrably good ones could grow obsolete.

Chicago's architecture has historically demonstrated ambivalence regarding "received" architectural expression. Utilitarian tendencies have dominated the priorities of its buildings and their planning, and its architects have generally been tentative in the application of style, as it is broadly understood. Exceptions can be found in the City Beautiful promised by the World's Columbian Exposition, which was more or less totalizing in its embrace of classicism as an endorsed language and methodology for both architecture and city planning, and the subsequent Plan of Chicago of 1909 by Burnham and Bennett. Their privileging of classicism and the buildings they inspired were met with either enthusiasm or disdain, depending on the audience. But not indifference.

Fig. 1. Competition proposal for a memorial to D. H. Burnham, "The Burnham Promontory," by Aric Lasher, 2009.

Sullivan sought liberation from what he found to be an irrelevant and indiscriminately applied cultural overlay while pursuing his urge to embroider nearly all surfaces and elements with ornamental efflorescence. Adler and Sullivan's work is now history, but it is *Chicago's* history. Chicago: a city that is architecturally quite specific but perceives itself as having liberated architecture from specificity. Where is the place today for a rich and varied city of conflict, a place for engagement of the divergent currents of persistence and rejection, each challenging and buttressing its opponent? Does such a place exist? Can these things reside side by side? I believe that they can. A more elastic understanding of classicism can unite, impart clarity, and relate opposing narratives. The Chicago canon got it right there, I think. Its grid of streets and frames can go naked or clothed. And these most American elements can be found in all modern cities.

A more elastic understanding of classicism can unite, impart clarity, and relate opposing narratives.

Isn't Chicago's distinctive modernism ultimately classical? Related parts, proportionally refined, with their origins in construction and assembly, legible and transparent in their arrangement, adaptable and easily accommodated to either ornamental embellishment or the abstract expression of construction, comprise the canon of "Chicagoism." Before the prodigal return to America—in the person of Mies—of modernist ideas first explored by Wright and his cohort and later digested by the European avant-garde, the engineer's "Chicago frame" was typically hung with representational ornament, though usually only as much as the service of propriety and speculative profit required. These exercises in style and embellishment were often naïve, brittle, bloodless, and lacking in conviction, in my estimation, but familiar motifs were found there for reasons of custom, expectation, or public affection.

Mies's inscrutable prisms and the work of his acolytes seemed to represent an impossible achievement: a fully realized system of principles that was applicable to all building problems and scales, with its own approach to construction, expression and spatiality. It was as if a single answer to many questions had emerged miraculously, in its adult state. These buildings were classical in their disciplinary rigor, their subjugation to order, clear relationship of form, space, and their constituent elements, expressed through an almost instantaneously evolved and refined language derived from, if often (like classicism) only imitative of, construction and assembly. And these principles could be taught, imitated, or transformed. What could be more classical? What was missing? We had everything we needed. Everything except the particular and the subjective, the memory of myth, mystery, and the vulgar sensualities and inherited refinements that gratify the greedy eye and receive its loving touch.

The experience of pure form can be exhilarating, and compelling in its promise of heroic originality, but can it satisfy all desires in all circumstances? Retreat to the world of the past denies us the spectacular unfolding of new experiences through new means, but must that be all there is, always? I wonder. It seems as if the persistent appeal and potency of forms that are, like human language, inherited and arbitrary, but describe a fuller world, challenge the notion of the absolute triumph of a self-correcting "style to end all styles."

In my personal pursuit of meaningful work, designing buildings and places that strive to resonate and survive the churn of time, change, and transformation, I take the broadest possible view. I am wary of some classicists' narrow boundaries, and I remain unmoved by the esoteric abstraction that encompasses so much of contemporary theorizing and practice. I am convinced that there is a small but important place for work that specifically addresses the potential of recognizable form enlisted in the service of either new, evolving, or persistent needs and specific identities. Circumstances in which historically derived expression is either appropriate or desired is deserving of a rigorous, creative, and vital engagement of the architect's art.

I have benefited from great mentors. Mentors whose affections straddled the rigors of their education in Chicago modernism, and the inexorable pull of things swept away or imprisoned by tidy, "zeitgeistian" boundaries. They sought reconciliation. I found this

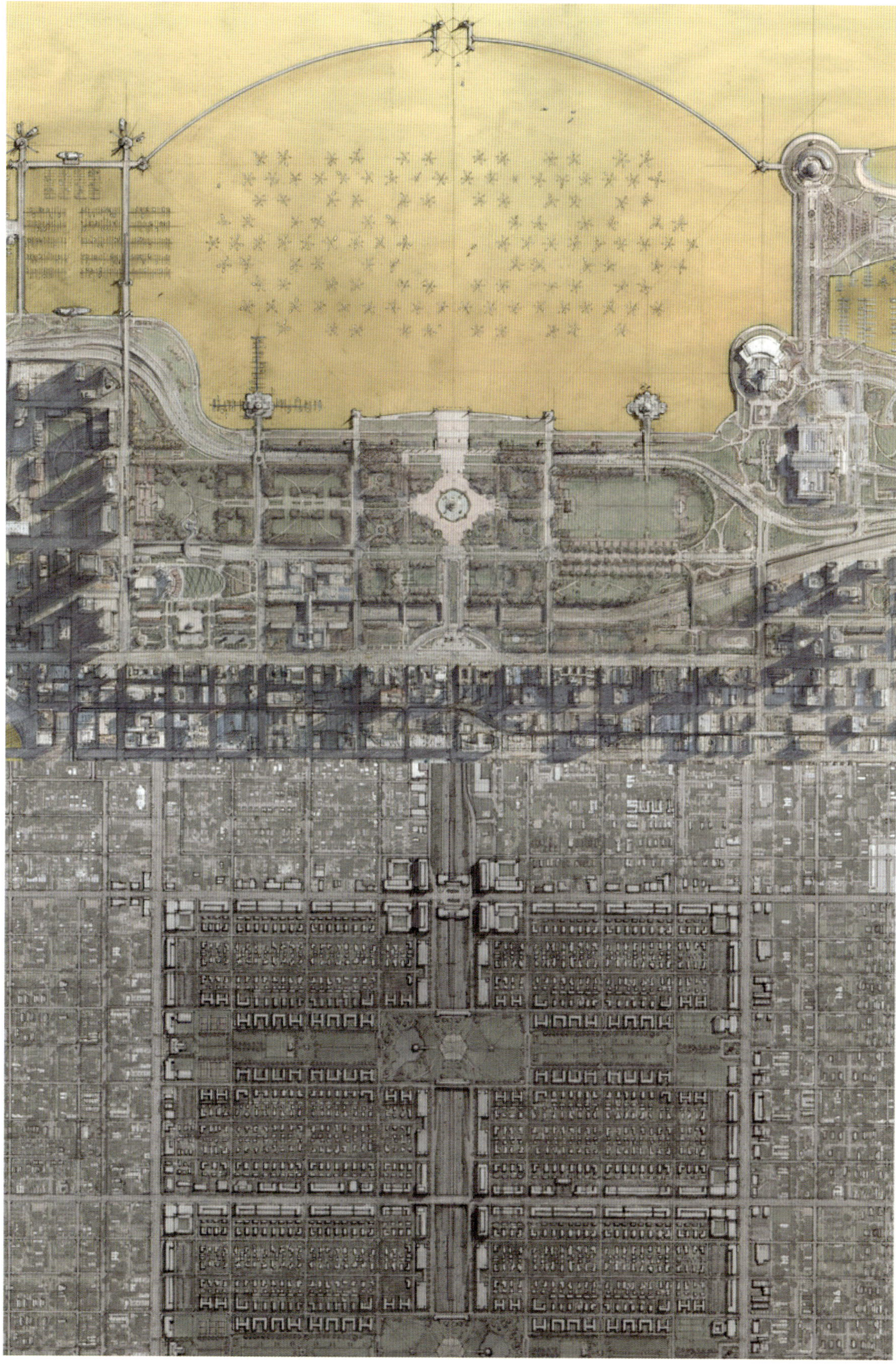

From *Plans of Chicago* by R. Samuel Roche and Aric Lasher (Chicago: Architects Research Foundation, 2010)

Fig. 2. Proposed improvements for Grant Park, Chicago, and typical quarter-section plans by Aric Lasher, 2009.

path to be compatible with my own yearnings, and it points toward a methodology that rewards with challenges and satisfaction, and is constantly born anew. In my office, common interests and methods provide a stable, if evolving, foundation for our practice, and though much of our work has been realized outside of the city, the lessons of the "Chicago way" are evident in the design of many of our buildings.

Chicago lacks the ostentation and voluptuary splendors of Paris or classical New York. But Chicago has something else—a seriousness and an underlying order, or at least it did, when architects paid attention to such things. This order undergirds the architecture of the city in whose grids Colin Rowe saw the defining element of a "modernist Florence," an order that relates its infrastructure, its plan, and its significant modern and pre-modern buildings. This order is the essential life blood of Chicago's homegrown classicism, the DNA of buildings demonstrative of this city's native technologies and lust for profit and utility, realized through the indigenous materials smelted and milled from Midwestern ore, fired from regional clay, or carved from Indiana's limestone. Here is a place that has evolved means that just might be capable of reconciling the usually segregated realms of persistent grammars and emerging methods.

The city that strove to transcend inherited histories has many of its own. They are what drew me here, offering something to embrace or reject as the case may be, but not to be ignored. During my Los Angeles years, spent inventing or evoking architectures as a set designer for the film industry, the late California architect Frank Israel, having seen some of my architectural work, declared that "even your modernist designs show a deep love for history." He was, I think, correct in his assessment. And in Chicago, modernism is just one of Chicago's histories.

I envy those architects who are never challenged by doubt, or who see beauty only in the orders, or endorse the genesis of meaningful form only in new and wholly unencumbered ways. These are the attributes Chicago wants to celebrate in its architects—no-nonsense, clearly positioned within the orderly scheme that is so often used to characterize the progress of Chicago architecture. A world in which all is alive at once is a messy place of conflict, promise, and fecundity. I embrace that world, and am confident in my belief that surrender to an unprejudiced love for architecture, not uncritical, but open and liberated from the exclusions of indoctrination and bias, can unleash tremendous possibility and inexpressible joy. And a path can be found in Chicago.

Fig. 3. Plan and elevation study for Bass Library entry pavilion, Yale University, by Aric Lasher, 2006.

Aric Lasher is president and director of design at HBRA Architects in Chicago, where his projects have included buildings for government, cultural, academic, and public institutions, residential projects, landscapes, and renovations and restorations of historic structures. In addition to his work in architecture, he has designed sets for numerous films, including *Minority Report, Pearl Harbor,* and *What Dreams May Come.* Lasher is a Fellow of the American Institute of Architects and serves on the boards of the Mies van der Rohe Society and the Society of Architectural Historians.

PROFESSIONAL PORTFOLIO

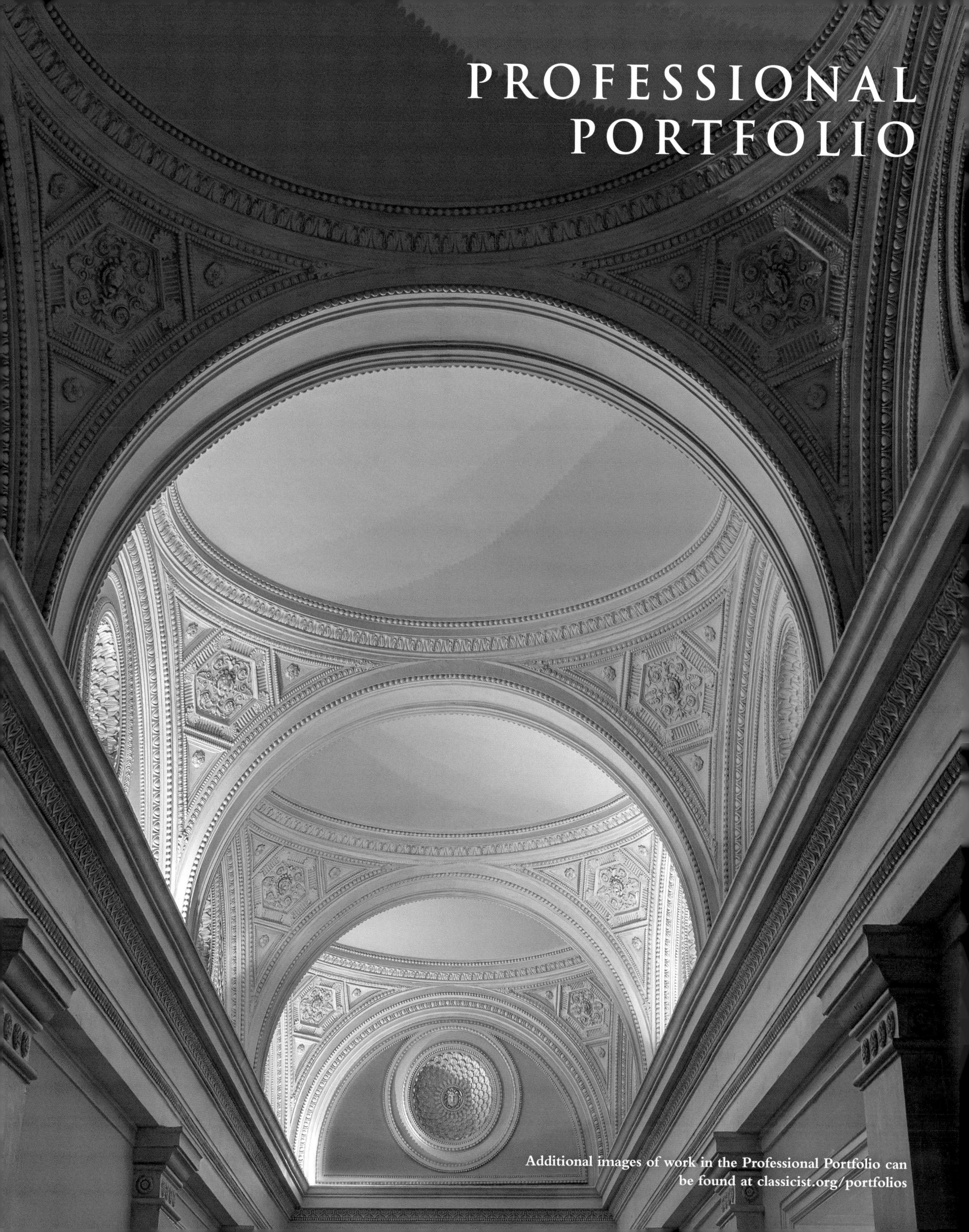

Additional images of work in the Professional Portfolio can be found at classicist.org/portfolios

Photo: Nathan Kirkman Photography

Classic Georgian Town House, Chicago
BBA Architects

Photo: SGW

Private Residence on School Street, Chicago
Sullivan, Goulette & Wilson Architects

Photo: © Bruce Van Inwegen

Private Residence, Chicago
Booth Hansen

Photo: Tony Soluri Photography

Georgian Town House in Lincoln Park, Chicago
Liederbach and Graham Architects

Photo: Hackley & Associates Architects, Inc.

Georgian House, Winnetka
Restoration Architect: Hackley & Associates Architects, Inc. Original Architect: David Adler

Photo: © 2019 James Caulfield

Ragdale, Lake Forest
Restoration Architect: Johnson Lasky Kindelin Architects Original Architect: Howard Van Doren Shaw

French Norman Style House, Lake Forest
Restoration Architect: Adrian Smith, FAIA Original Architect: David Adler

North Shore Mediterranean House, Winnetka
Restoration Architect: Morgante Wilson Architects Original Architect: Clark & Walcott

Photo: Tony Soluri

Palladian Style Guest House, Glencoe
Gibbons, Fortman & Associates

Photo: Kathleen Page

Lake Shore Residence, Evanston
Konstant Architecture & Planning

Photo: Jon Miller © Hedrich-Blessing

Private Residence, Winnetka
Booth Hansen

Photo: Tony Soluri Photography

Mediterranean Villa on the Shores of Lake Michigan, Lake Forest
Liederbach and Graham Architects

House on Sleight Street, Naperville
Derrick Architecture

Farmhouse, Lake Bluff
Edward Deegan Architects

Photo: SGW

Private Residence on Greenview Avenue, Chicago
Sullivan, Goulette & Wilson Architects

Photo: Dave Burk/Hedrich-Blessing

Arts and Crafts Style House, Evanston
Stuart Cohen & Julie Hacker Architects LLC

Photo: Francis Son

Chestnut Row Homes, Chicago
Booth Hansen

Photo: SGW

Grant Place Townhomes, Chicago
Sullivan, Goulette & Wilson Architects

Photo: James Caulfield for Robert A.M. Stern Architects

One Bennett Park, Chicago
Robert A.M. Stern Architects

Photo: Matt Cashore/University of Notre Dame

Walsh Family Hall, University of Notre Dame
John Simpson Architects

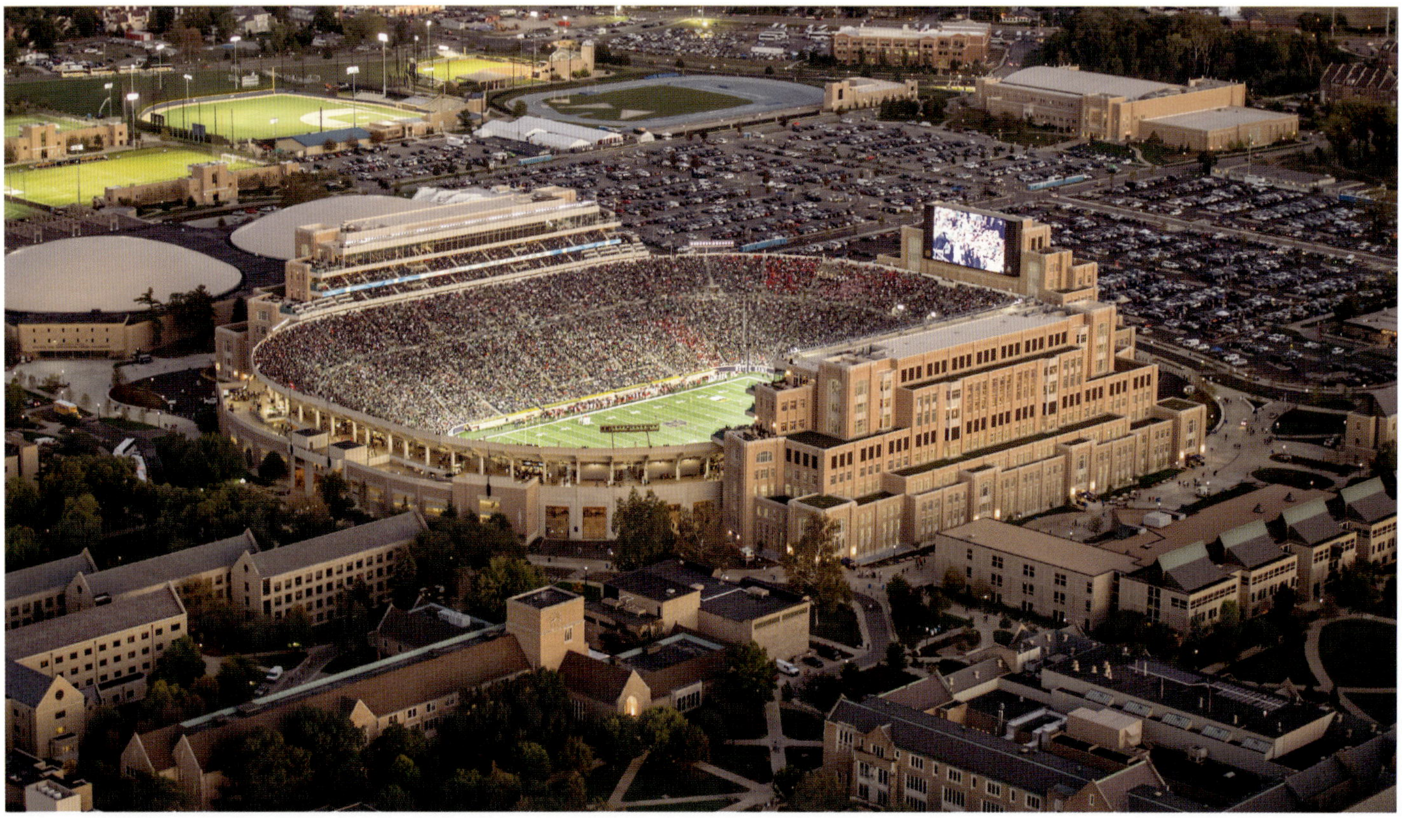

Photo: Barbara Johnston/University of Notre Dame

Campus Crossroads Project, Stadium with Academic and Student Life Additions, University of Notre Dame
The SLAM Collaborative

Photo: Steve Hall © Hall + Merrick Photographers

Jenkins and Nanovic Halls, University of Notre Dame
HBRA Architects, Inc.

Photo: Francis Dzikowski / Otto for Robert A.M. Stern Architects

Stayer Center for Executive Education, Mendoza College of Business, University of Notre Dame
Robert A.M. Stern Architects

Photo: Tony Soluri Photography

Mundelein Hall, University of Saint Mary of the Lake
Architect of Record: Bureau | AD Design Architect: Thomas Norman Rajkovich Architect, Ltd.

Photo: Barry Rustin Photography

Buffalo Grove Bank & Trust, Buffalo Grove
Melichar Architects

Photo: Werner Straube

Private Women's Club, Chicago
Restoration Architect and Interior Design: Craig & Company   Original Architect: Philip Maher

Photo: Nicholas James

Chicago Union Station-Burlington Room, Chicago
Restoration Architect: Goettsch Partners, with murals by EverGreene Architectural Arts   Original Architect: Graham, Anderson, Probst & White

Photo: Tony Soluri Photography

Garden Folly, Lake Forest
Liederbach and Graham Architects after Samuel McIntyre

Photo: Matt Cashore

The Morrison Family Education & Outreach Pavilion at the Notre Dame Linked Experimental Ecosytem Facility
Buccellato Design, LLC

ACADEMIC PORTFOLIO

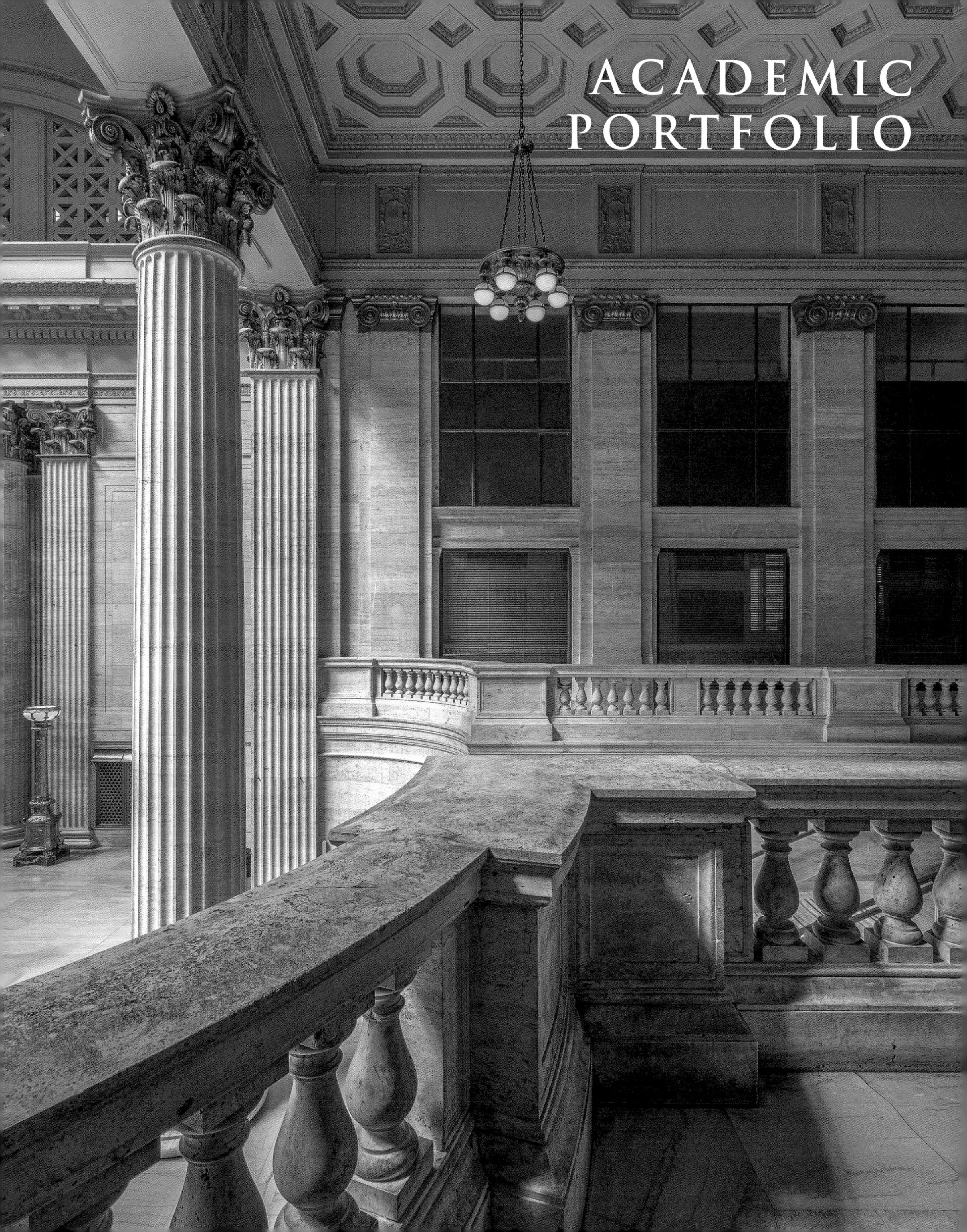

UNIVERSITY OF NOTRE DAME

Notre Dame, Indiana

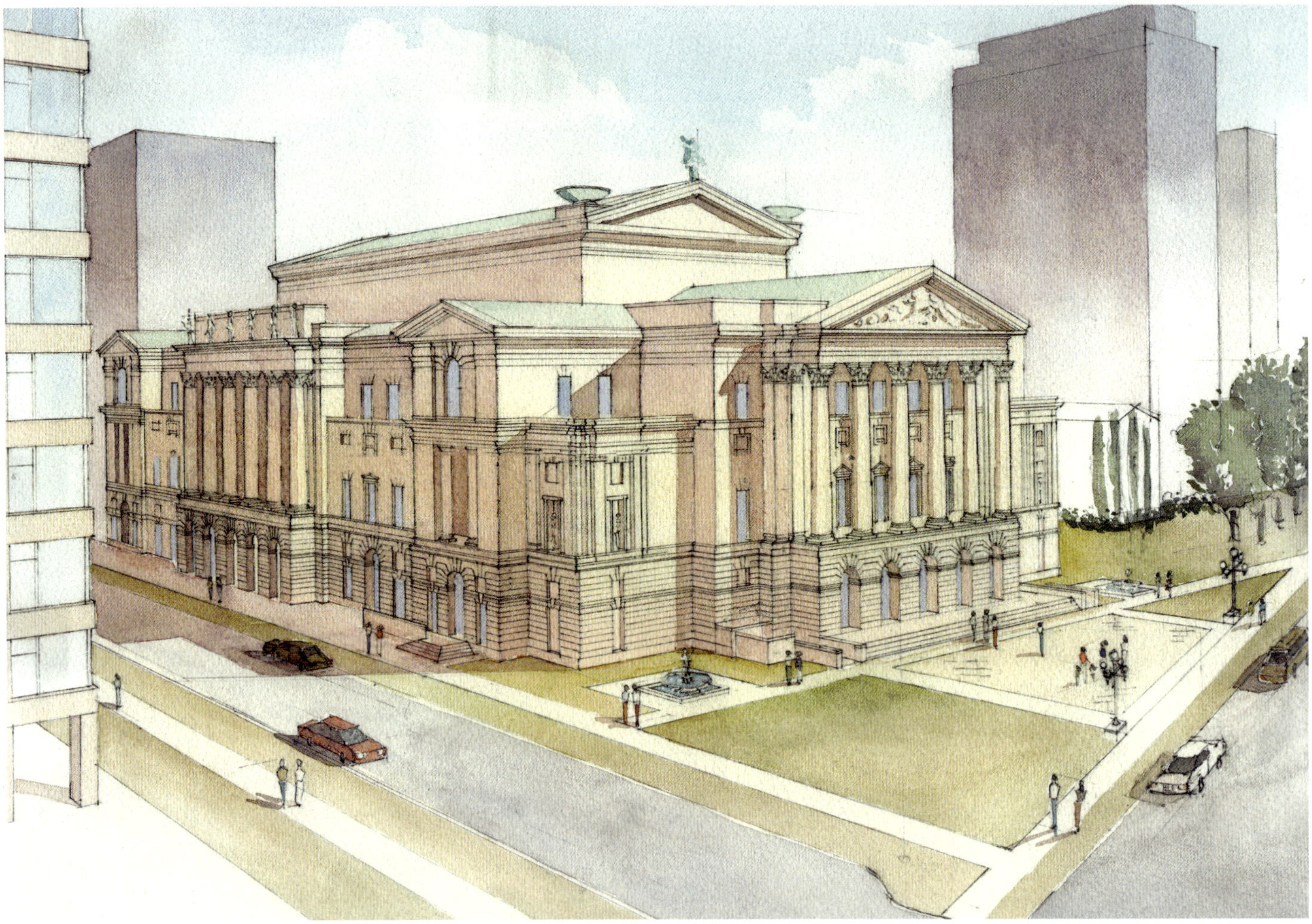

Symphony Hall in Lincoln Park, Chicago, Illinois
Julian Murphy, 1st Year Graduate; Instructor: Duncan Stroik

Institute of Dunhuang Arts, Beijing, China
Xiaoyun Margaret Zhang, 2nd Year Graduate; Instructor: Michael Lykoudis

UNIVERSITY OF NOTRE DAME

Notre Dame, Indiana

Roman Villa and Gardens, Rome, Italy
Joseph M. Faccibene, 3rd Year; Instructor: Ettore Maria Mazzola

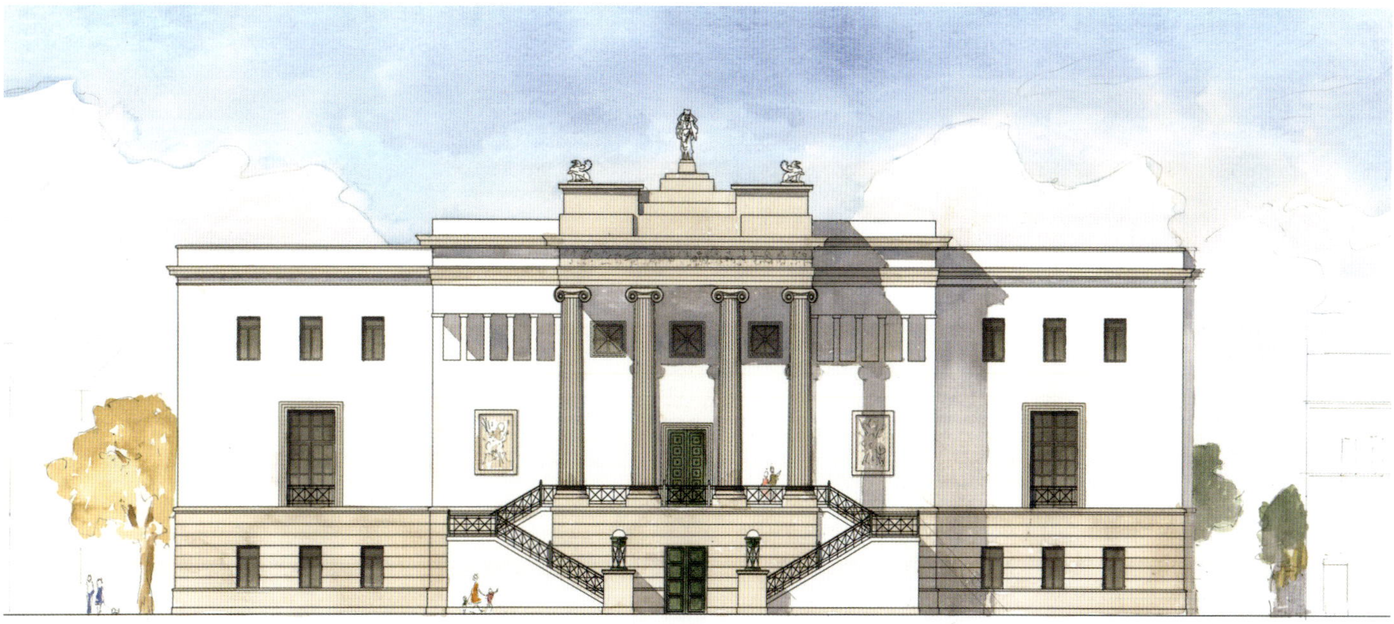

Archaeological Museum, Nauplion, Greece
Stephen Dudro, 1st Year Graduate; Instructor: Richard Economakis

UNIVERSITY OF NOTRE DAME

Notre Dame, Indiana

House in the Manner of C.F.A. Voysey, Lake District, England
Alexandria Gordon, 5th Year; Instructor: Aimee Bucccellato

Museum of the History of Segregation, Charlottesville, Virginia
Christian Cullinan, 5th Year; Instructor: Aimee Buccellato

Ampthill Estate Terrace House, London, England
Alex Athenson, 2nd Year Graduate; Instructor: Richard Economakis

AUBURN UNIVERSITY

Auburn, Alabama

Analysis, Kentworthy Hall, Marion, Alabama
Tanner Rose Harden, 3rd Year; Instructor: Richard Hudgens

Analysis, St. Luke's Episcopal Church, Selma, Alabama
Henry Savoie, 3rd Year; Instructor: Richard Hudgens

MISSISSIPPI STATE UNIVERSITY

Starkville, Mississippi

Classical School, Starkville, Mississippi
Meredith Anne Hutto, 4th Year; Instructor: Fred Esenwein

CATHOLIC UNIVERSITY OF AMERICA
Washington, D.C.

Annapolis Gateway, Annapolis, Maryland
Patrick Suarez, 4th Year; Instructor: James McCrery

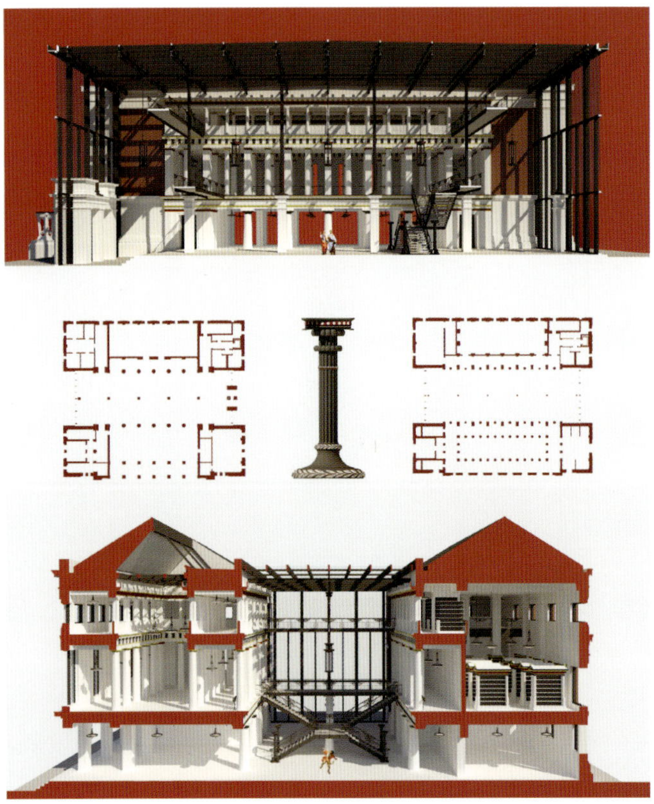

Democracy of the Library, Clarksburg, Maryland
Patrick Suarez and Jacob Chase, 4th Year; Instructor: Christopher J. Howard

CATHOLIC UNIVERSITY OF AMERICA

Washington, D.C.

The Annapolis Market, Annapolis, Maryland
Tommy Vince, 1st Year Graduate; Instructor: James McCrery

Library, Clarksburg, Maryland
Ryan Gebhart, 2nd Year Graduate; Instructor: James McCrery

DREXEL UNIVERSITY
Philadelphia, Pennsylvania

Beaux-Arts High-Rise
Abraham Calhoun, 2nd Year

ANDREWS UNIVERSITY
Berrien Springs, Michigan

El Nexo Martín Peña, San Juan, Puerto Rico
Nathan Bolkovic, 5th Year, Instructors:
Andrew von Maur and Troy Homenchuck

ARCHITECTURAL ASSOCIATION
London, England

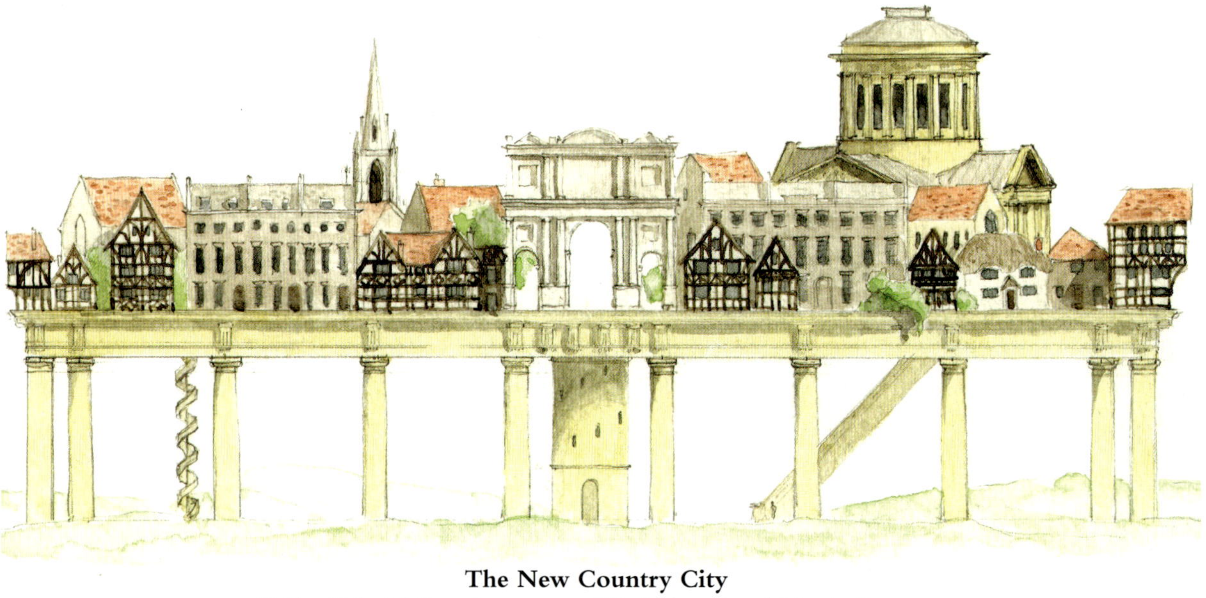

The New Country City
Zi Ken Toh, 4th Year; Instructors: Miraj Ahmed and Martin Jameson

BENEDICTINE COLLEGE

Atchison, Kansas

The Run for the Roses
Adele Bischel, 3rd Year; Instructor: John Haigh

Proposal for a Penn-Hudson Elevated Walkway, New York, New York
Matthew Bridge, Margaret Jones, Mary Leihy, Michael Miller, Dalton Smith, John Weber, 3rd Year; Instructor: John Haigh

UNIVERSITY OF COLORADO

Denver, Colorado

Clear Creek Main Street, Adams County, Colorado
Zac Rott, 1st Year Graduate; Instructor: Keith Loftin

VIRGINIA COMMONWEALTH UNIVERSITY

Richmond, Virginia

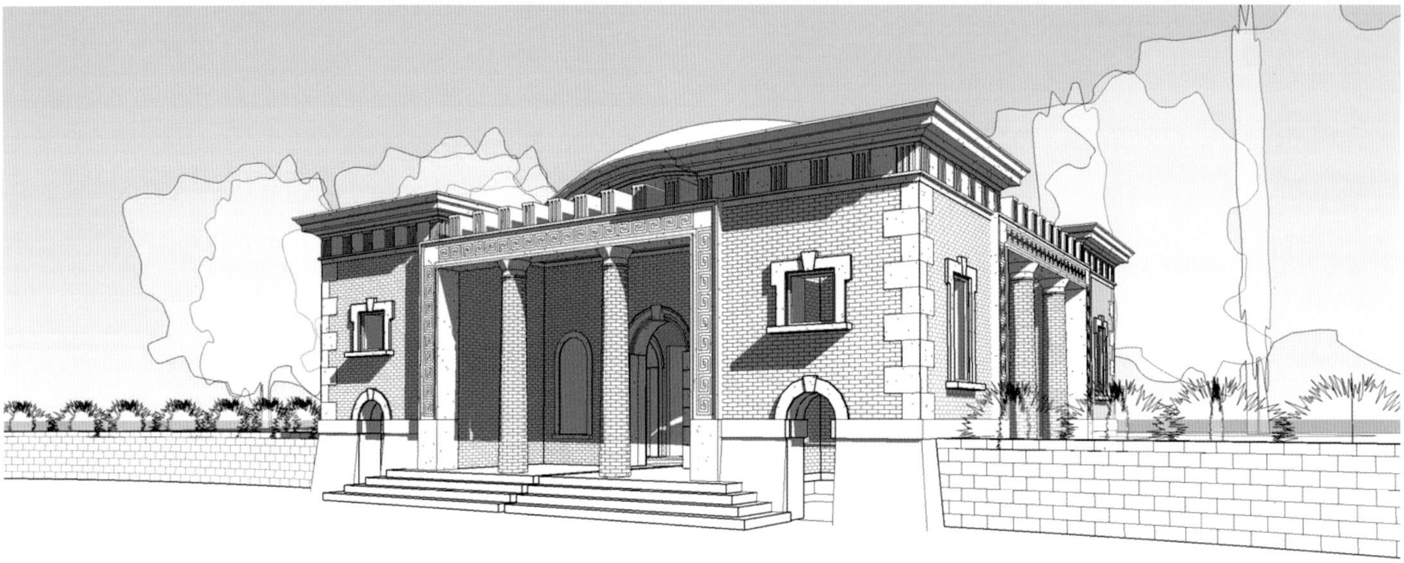

Nymphaeum
Nathan Varble, 1st Year Graduate; Instructor: Peter Hodson

YALE UNIVERSITY

New Haven, Connecticut

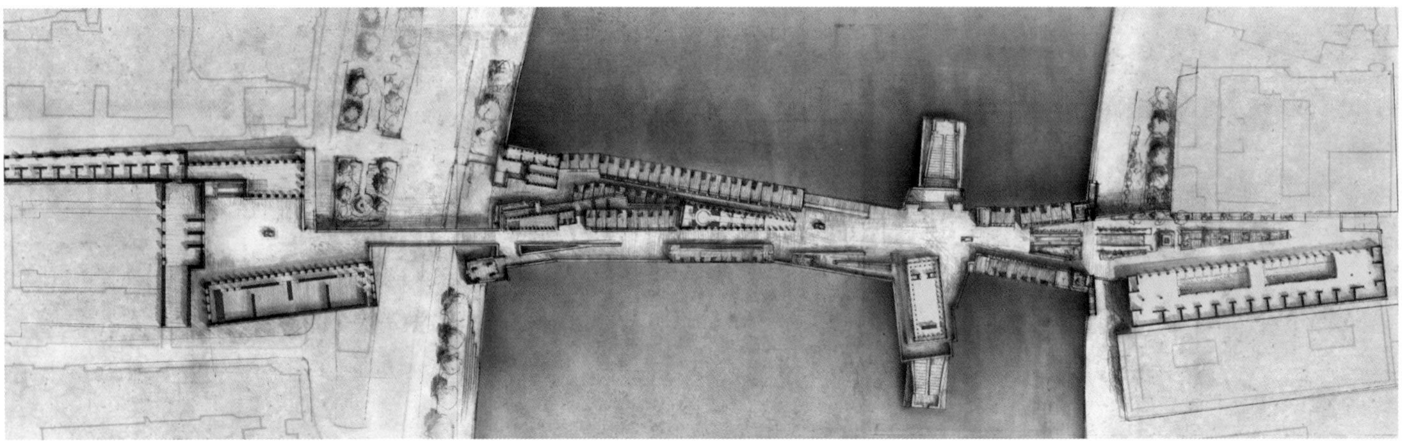

High Street Bridge, London, England
Jincy George Kunnatharayil and Jerome Tryon, 2nd Year Graduate; Instructors: George Knight and Paul Florian

UNIVERSITY OF MIAMI

Coral Gables, Florida

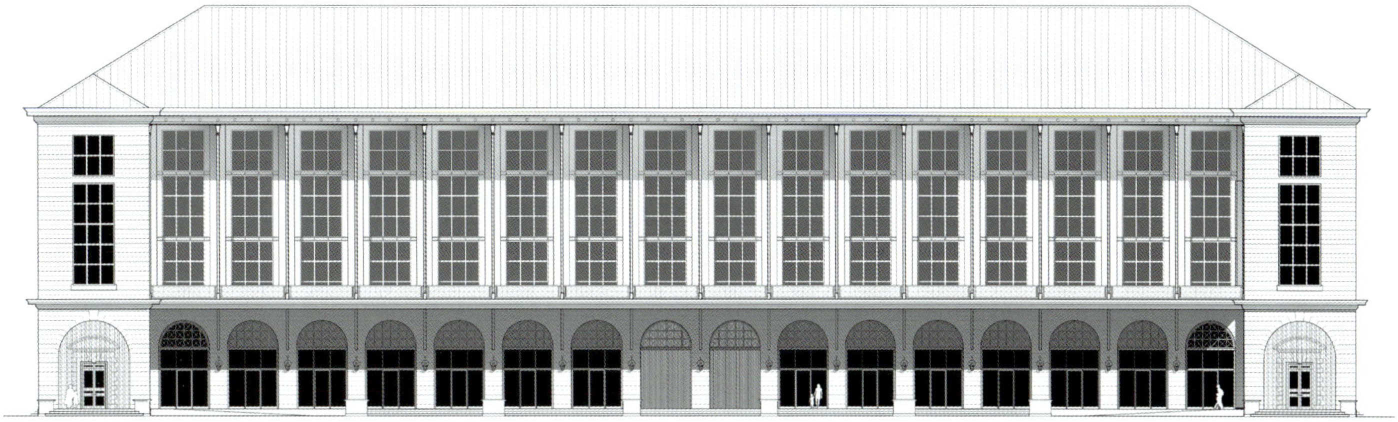

Aquatic Center, Miami, Florida
Cecilia McCammon, 2nd Year; Instructor: Oscar Machado

KTH ROYAL INSTITUTE OF TECHNOLOGY

Stockholm, Sweden

Memory Forum, Stockholm, Sweden
Liam Gordon Price, 5th Year; Instructor: Ian Alexander

KINGSTON SCHOOL OF ART

London, England

Restaurant, Syracuse, Italy

Anthony A. Fitheoglou, 1st Year Graduate; Instructors: Timothy Smith and Jonathan Taylor

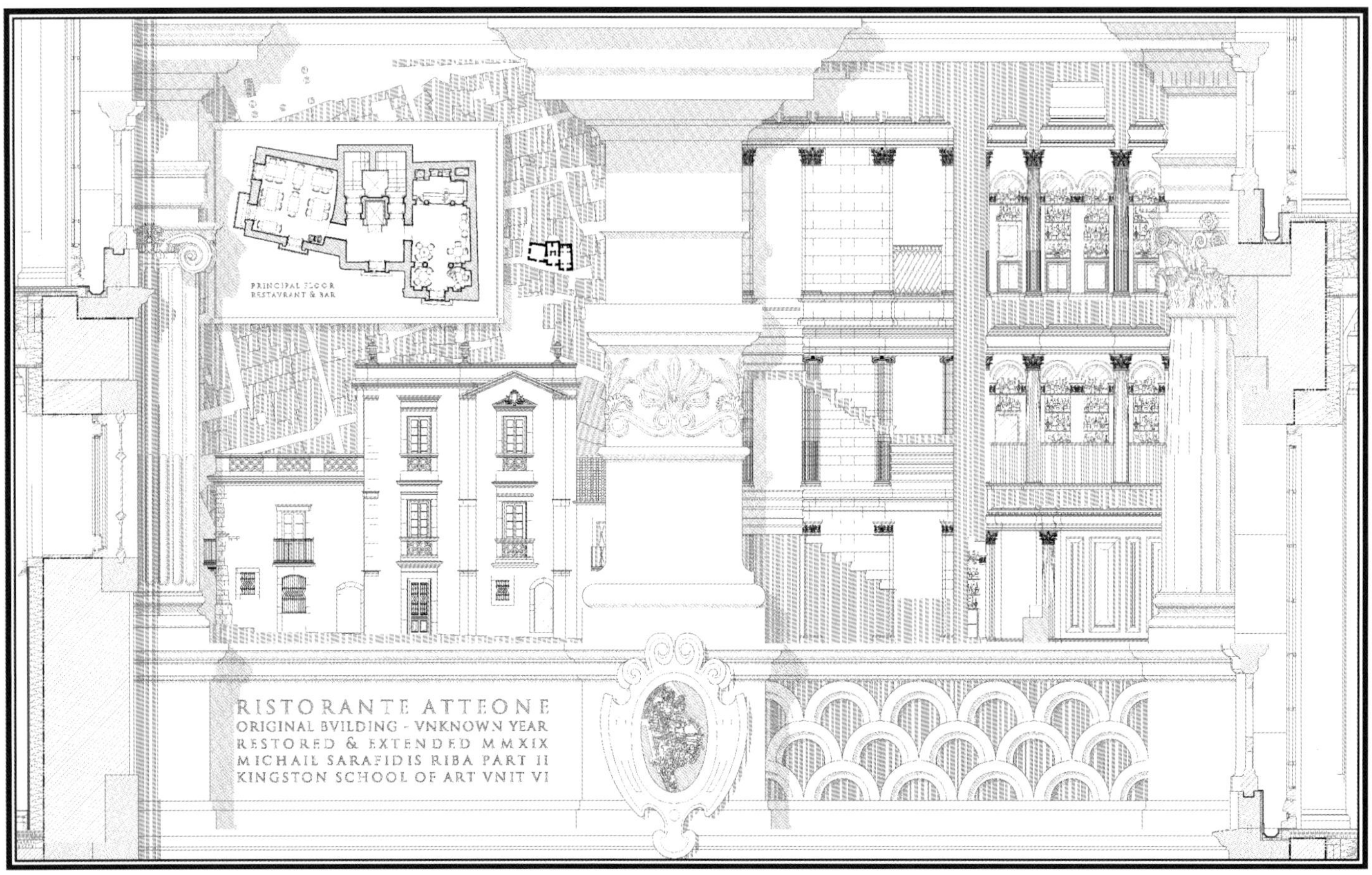

Restaurant, Syracuse, Italy

Michail Sarafidis, 5th Year; Instructors: Timothy Smith and Jonathan Taylor

KINGSTON SCHOOL OF ART

London, England

Restaurant, Syracuse, Italy
Greg Oleniacz, 2nd Year Graduate; Instructors: Timothy Smith and Jonathan Taylor

Greek Revival Fragments
Marwa Al-Khudairy, Sonal Bajaria, Peter Canelle-Dance, Peter Folland, Parisa Ghorani, Tsz Lok Hsu, Christodoula Ioannou, Kate Ivinson, Tabir Momin Khan, Puisan Lee, Michelle Mujakachi, Bradlee Mulroe-Sanders, Greg Oleniacz, Guiditta Pedace, Michail Sarafidis, Shpetim Serani, Fatima Tahan, Marian Twenefoo, Aleksandra Zenfa; 4th and 5th Years; Instructors: Timothy Smith, Jonathan Taylor, Alexander Gore

INTBAU

Engelsburg Summer School in Classical Architecture, Engelsburg, Sweden

House, Jaca, Spain
Irene Molnar;
Instructor: José Baganha

Nobel Center, Stockholm, Sweden
Diana Yu; Instructors: Jonathan Taylor and Timothy Smith

Marvão Traditional Architecture Summer School, Portugal

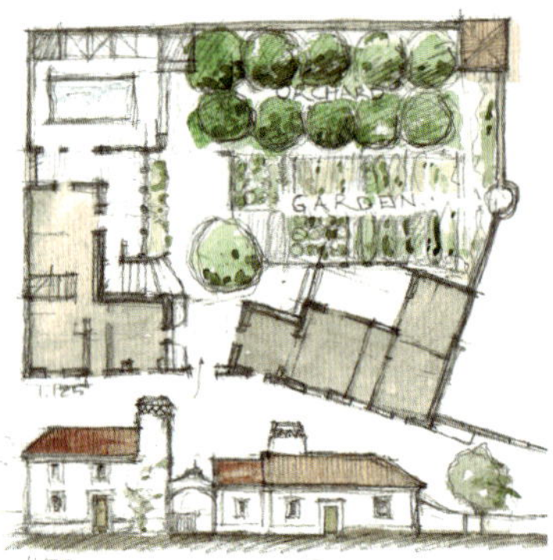

(UPPER LEFT) **Typical Casa of the Alentejo Region, Ribeira of Beirã, Portugal,** Andrew Moneyheffer; (UPPER RIGHT) **Proposal for Town Hall, Beirã, Portugal,** Molly Jorden and Natalie Stenger; (ABOVE) **Proposed Square for the Arrabalde area of Beirã, Portugal,** Deyglis Castillo, Saniya Malhotra, Emilio Roldán Zamarrón, Alexandra Scupin, Mario Vides; Instructors: Frank Martínez, Christopher Miller, Douglas Duany, Alejandro García Hermida

INSTITUTE OF CLASSICAL ARCHITECTURE & ART

Intensive in Classical Architecture: Los Angeles

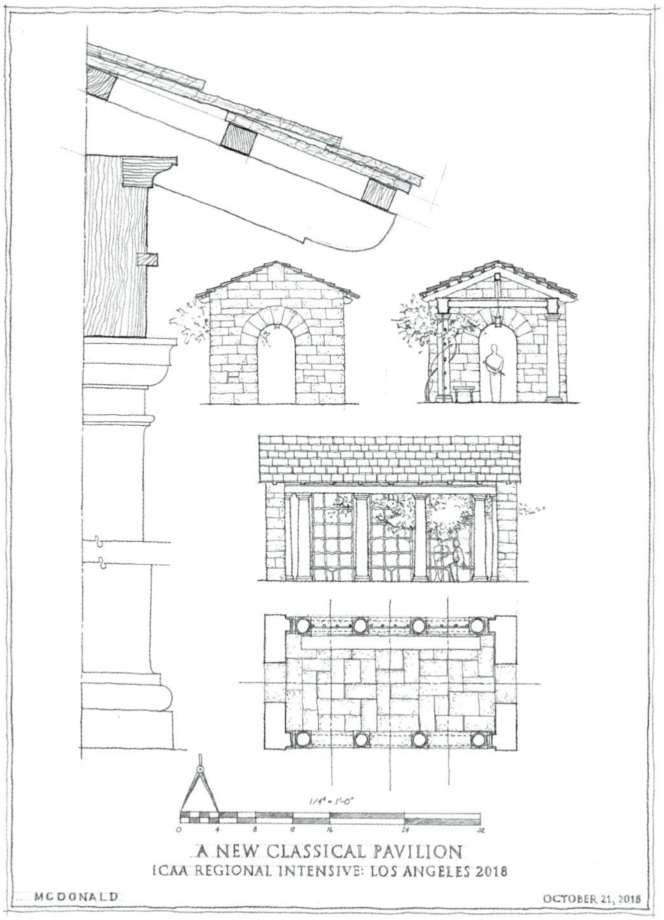

Continuing Education

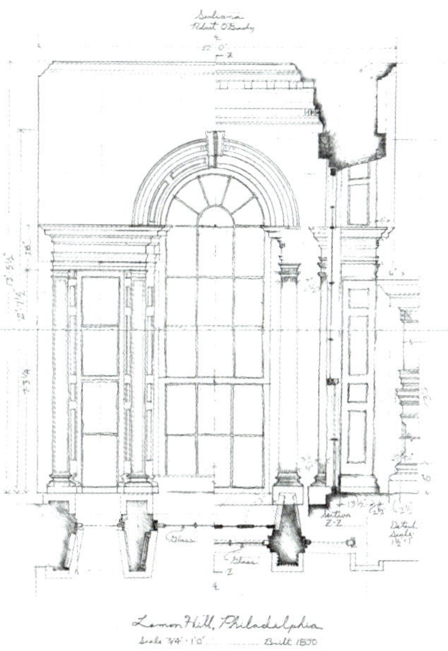

New Classical Pavilion, Los Angeles, California: (UPPER LEFT) Stephanie Jazmines; (UPPER RIGHT) Donald McDonald; Instructors: Michael Mesko and Chris Eiland; (LOWER LEFT) **Architectural Rendering in Wash,** Eric Easterling; Instructor: David Genther; (LOWER RIGHT) **Lemon Hill, Philadelphia, Pennsylvania,** Robert O'Grady; Instructors: Stephen Chrisman and Martin Burns

Christopher H. Browne Williamsburg Drawing Tour

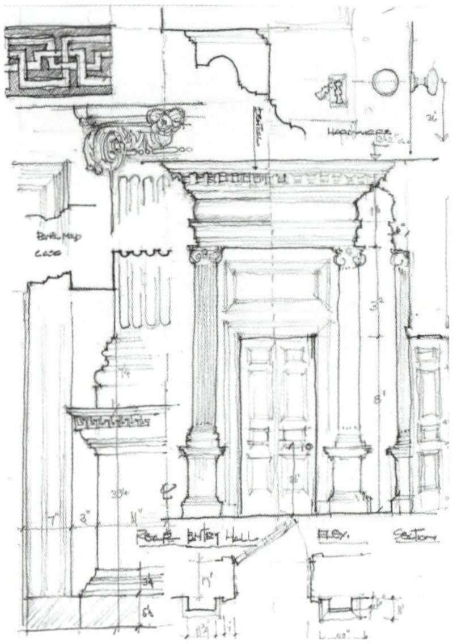

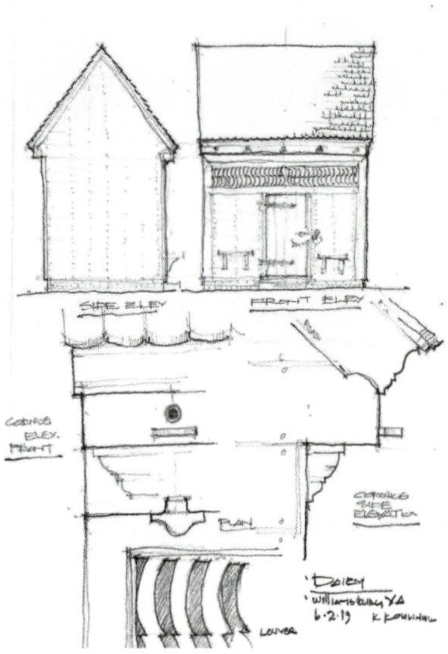

Christopher H. Browne Paris Drawing Tour

Summer Studio in Classical Architecture

(UPPER LEFT) **Robert Carter House, Williamsburg, Virginia,** and (UPPER RIGHT) **Study of a Dairy House, Williamsburg, Virginia,** Kevin Ohlinger; Instructor: Stephen Chrisman and Martin Burns; (MIDDLE LEFT) **Place des Vosges, Paris, France,** Jacques Levet; (MIDDLE) **Petit Trianon, Versailles, France,** Jori Colarusso; (MIDDLE RIGHT) **Studio Exercise,** Josh Pickering; Instructors: Kahlil Hamady and Leslie-Jon Vickory; (LOWER LEFT) **Wash Rendering,** Julie Chandler, University of Colorado Denver; Instructor: David Genther; (LOWER RIGHT) **Light and Shade Study,** Ian Reilly, Benedictine College; Instructor: Giuseppe Mazzone

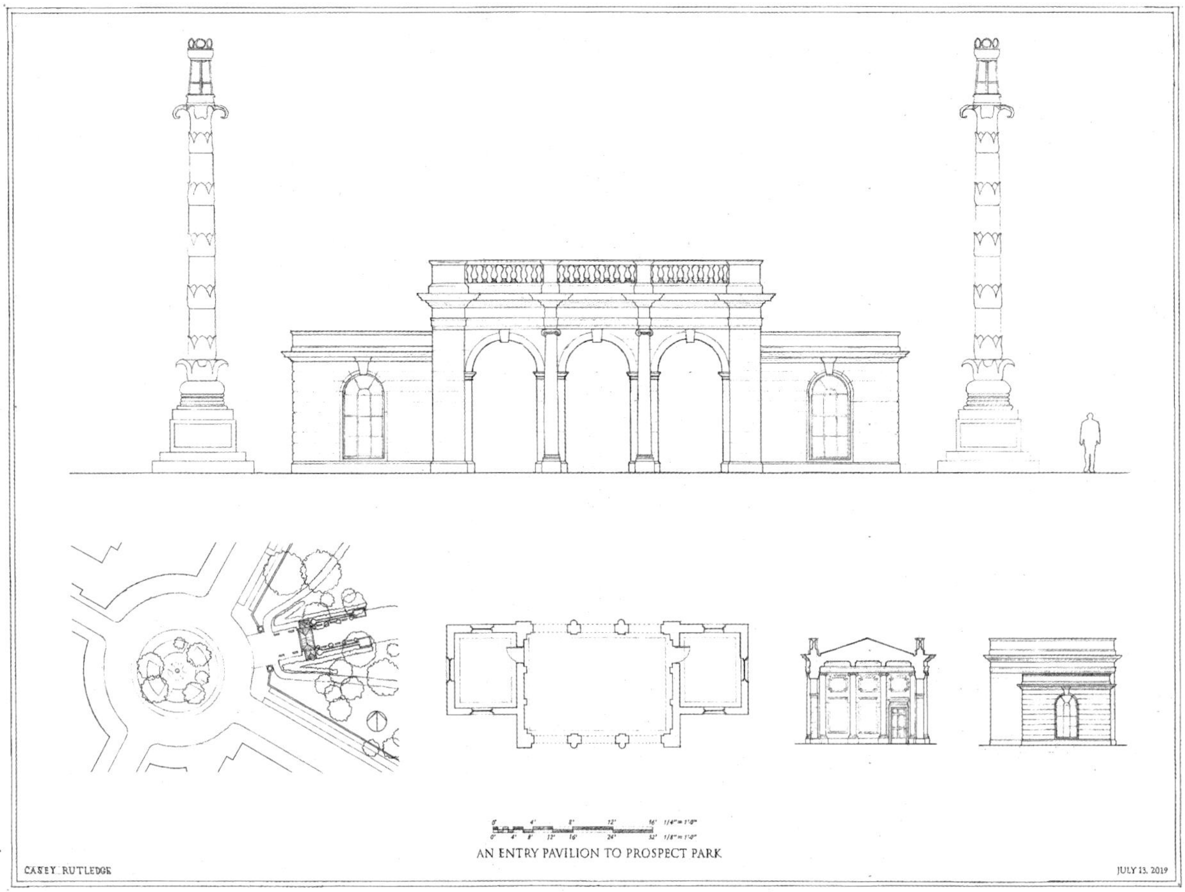

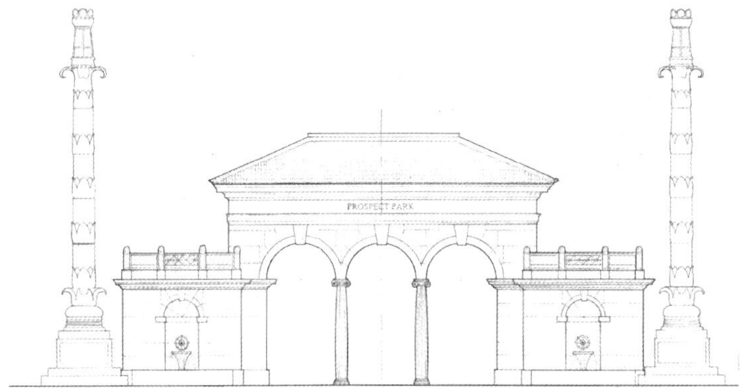

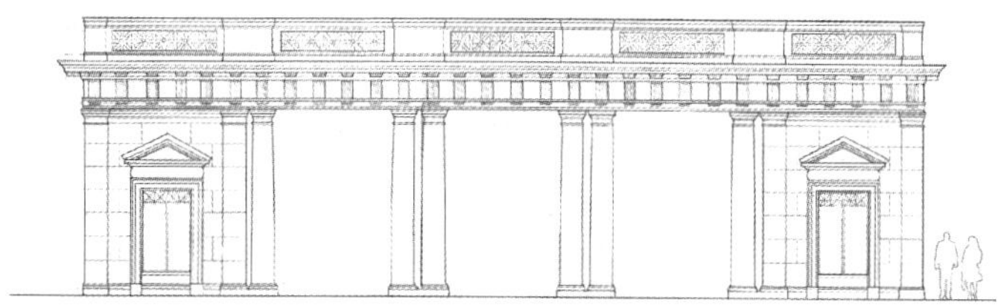

Entry Pavilion to Prospect Park, Brooklyn, New York: (TOP) Casey Rutledge, Catholic University of America; (MIDDLE LEFT) Gary Glinsey, Hampton University; (MIDDLE RIGHT) Andre Johnson, University of Cincinnati; (LOWER LEFT) Evan Markley, Catholic University of America; (LOWER RIGHT) Jacob McCarthy, Princeton University; Instructors: Michael Mesko, Mark Santrach, Javier Perez

BEAUX-ARTS ACADEMY
Provo, Utah

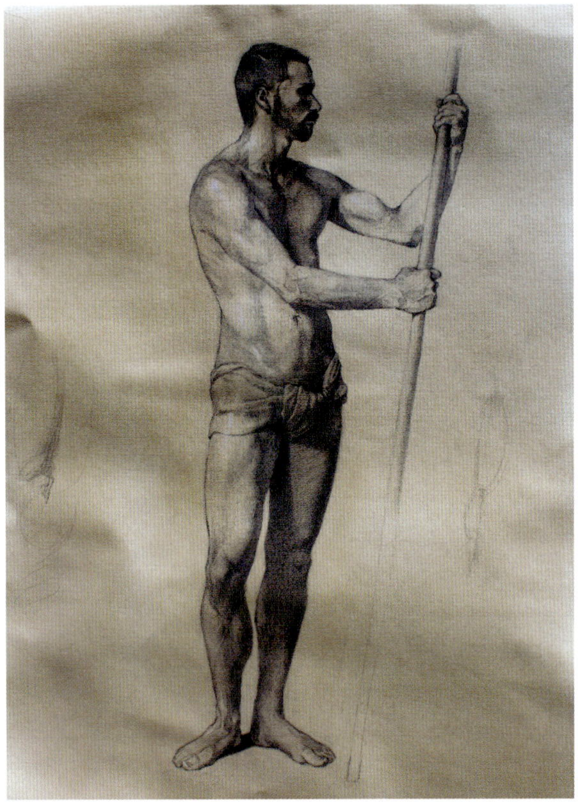

Drawing from the Live Model
Jeanette Lee, 2nd Year Graduate; Instructor: Joseph Brickey

ACADEMY OF CLASSICAL DESIGN
Southern Pines, North Carolina

Ariadne
Rodney Wilkinson; Instructor: D. Jeffrey Mims

ACADEMY OF CLASSICAL DESIGN
Southern Pines, North Carolina

Ornament Study
Ali Sexton; Instructor: D. Jeffrey Mims

Ornament Study
Peter Daniel; Instructor: D. Jeffrey Mims

Ornament Study
Lane Koster; Instructor D. Jeffrey Mims

BIBLIOGRAPHY

SELECTED BIBLIOGRAPHY

ON CHICAGO ARCHITECTURE

In 1924, *Architectural Record* ran a series called "The Library of the Architect" for which it asked a number of nationally known architects to provide a list of must-own books on architecture. When the Art Institute of Chicago began acquiring the books that would become the Burnham Architecture Library and later the Ryerson and Burnham Libraries, the director of the Art Institute, in 1905, asked Daniel Burnham for a list of twenty-five to thirty titles. The same request was made of Howard Van Doren Shaw, James Gamble Rogers, Charles Frost, Alfred Granger, Solomon Beman, Louis Sullivan, Irving Pond, and Dwight Perkins. Shaw, a trustee of the Art Institute and a contributor to *Architectural Record*'s series, was put in charge of purchasing books, and would leave his own extensive library to the Art Institute. Funded by a $50,000 behest, made in 1912, from the estate of Daniel Burnham, the Ryerson and Burnham Libraries are considered today, along with the RIBA Library in London and Columbia University's Avery Library, to be one of the great architectural libraries of the world.

In keeping with this tradition, the editors have asked a number of architects, historians, and educators for their lists of books on Chicago architecture. Those who responded were Thomas Rajkovich, William Westfall, Robert Bruggeman, John Zukowsky, Jeanne Sylvester, and Nathaniel Parks. The following list focuses on Chicago's classical era, although it includes some texts that also reflect Chicago's place in the history of twentieth-century architecture.

Appelbaum, Stanley. *The Chicago World's Fair of 1893: A Photographic Record.* New York: Dover Publications, 1980.

___. *Spectacle in the White City: The Chicago 1893 World's Fair.* Mineola, NY: Calla Editions, 2009.

Arnold, C. D., and H. D. Higinbotham. *Official Views of the World's Columbian Exposition. Chicago*: Press Chicago Photo-gravure Co., 1893.

Benjamin, Susan, and Stuart Cohen. *Great Houses of Chicago 1871–1921.* New York: Acanthus Press. 2008.

Berger, Miles L. *They Built Chicago: Entrepreneurs Who Shaped a Great City's Architecture.* Chicago: Bonus Books, 1992.

Block, Jean. *Hyde Park Houses: An Informal History*, 1856–1910. Chicago: University of Chicago Press, 1978.

Bluestone, Daniel. *Constructing Chicago.* New Haven, CT: Yale University Press, 1993.

Bolotin, Norman, and Christine Laing. *The World's Columbian Exposition: The Chicago World's Fair of 1893.* Champaign, IL: University of Illinois Press, 2002.

Bruegmann, Robert. *Holabird & Roche/ Holabird & Root: An Illustrated Catalog of Works 1880–1940.* New York: Garland Publishing, in cooperation with the Chicago Historical Society, 1991.

___. *The Architects and the City: Holabird & Roche of Chicago, 1880–1918.* Chicago: University of Chicago Press, 1997.

Burg, David F. *Chicago's White City of 1893.* Lexington, KY: University Press of Kentucky, 1976.

Burnham, Daniel H., and Edward H. Bennett. *Plan of Chicago.* Edited by Charles Moore. New York: Princeton Architectural Press, 1993. Originally published in 1909 by the Commercial Club of Chicago.

Chappell, Sally A. Kitt. *Architecture and Planning of Graham, Anderson, Probst and White, 1912–1936: Transforming Tradition.* Chicago: University of Chicago Press, 1992.

Cohen, Stuart. *Inventing the New American House: Howard Van Doren Shaw, Architect.* New York: The Monacelli Press, 2015.

Cohen, Stuart, and Susan Benjamin. *North Shore Chicago: Houses of the Lakefront Suburbs, 1890–1940.* New York: Acanthus Press, 2004.

Cohen, Stuart, with Stanley Tigerman. *Chicago Architects.* Chicago: Swallow Press, 1976.

Condit, Carl W. *Chicago 1910–29: Building, Planning, and Urban Technology. Chicago*: University of Chicago Press, 1973.

___. *Chicago 1930–70: Building, Planning, and Urban Technology.* Chicago: University of Chicago Press, 1974.

___. *Chicago School of Architecture: A History of Commercial and Public Building in the Chicago Area, 1875–1925.* Chicago: University of Chicago Press, 1964.

Coventry, Kim, Daniel Meyer, and Arthur H. Miller. *Classic Country Estates of Lake Forest: Architecture and Landscape Design 1856–1940.* New York: W. W. Norton & Co., 2003.

Coventry, Kim, and Arthur H. Miller. *Walter Frazier and Rafery, Orr & Fairbank Architects: Houses of Chicago's North Shore, 1924–1970.* Lake Forest, IL: Lake Forest-Lake Bluff Historical Society, 2009.

Dart, Susan. *Market Square: Lake Forest, Illinois.* Lake Forest, IL: Lake Forest-Lake Bluff Historical Society, 1984.

Davis, Susan O'Connor. *Chicago's Historic Hyde Park.* Chicago: University of Chicago Press, 2013.

Di Cola, Joseph M., and David Stone. *Chicago's 1893 World's Fair.* Charleston, SC: Arcadia Publishing, 2012.

Draper, Joan E. *Edward Bennett: Architect and City Planner 1874–1954.* Chicago: University of Chicago Press, 1982.

Drury, John. *Old Chicago Houses.* New York: Bonanza Books, 1941.

Ebner, Michael H. *Creating Chicago's North Shore: A Suburban History.* Chicago: University of Chicago Press, 1988.

Eisenschmidt, Alexander, and Jonathan Mekinda, eds. *Chicagoisms: The City as Catalyst for Architectural Speculation.* Zurich: Park Books, 2013.

Ericsson, Henry. *Sixty Years a Builder.* Chicago: A. Kroch & Son, 1942.

Gilbert, Paul T., et al. *Chicago and Its Makers: A Narrative of Events from the Day of the First White Man to the Inception of the Second World's Fair.* Chicago: Felix Mendelsohn, 1929.

Graf, John. *Chicago's Mansions.* Charleston, SC: Arcadia Publishing, 2004.

Graham, Ernest. *The Architectural Work of Graham, Anderson, Probst & White and their Predecessors D. H. Burnham & Co. and Graham Burnham & Co.* London: B. T. Batsford, 1933.

Granger, Alfred. *Tribune Tower Competition: The International Competition for a New Administration Building for the Chicago Tribune.* Chicago: Tribune Company, 1923.

Greene, Virginia A. *The Architecture of Howard Van Doren Shaw.* Chicago: Chicago Review Press, 1998.

Harris, Neil. *Chicago Apartments: A Century of Lakefront Luxury.* New York: Acanthus Press, 2004.

Hasbrouck, Wilbert R. *The Chicago Architectural Club, Prelude to the Modern.* New York: The Monacelli Press, 2005.

Hines, Thomas S. *Burnham of Chicago: Architect and Planner.* New York: Oxford University Press, 1974.

Hoffmann, Donald. *The Architecture of John Wellborn Root.* Baltimore: Johns Hopkins University Press, 1973.

Johnson, Donald Leslie. *Frank Lloyd Wright: The Early Years.* New York: Routledge, 2017.

Landau, Sarah. P. B. *Wight: Architect, Contractor and Critic, 1838–1925.* Chicago: The Art Institute of Chicago, 1981.

Leslie, Thomas. *Chicago Skyscrapers, 1971–1934.* Champaign, IL: University of Illinois Press, 2013.

Lowe, David. *Lost Chicago.* Boston: Houghton Mifflin Company, 1975.

Manson, Grant Carpenter. *Frank Lloyd Wright to 1910: The First Golden Age.* New York: Van Nostrand Reinhold Co., 1958.

Mayer, Harold M., and Richard C. Wade. *Growth of a Metropolis.* Chicago: University of Chicago Press, 1969.

McNamara, Denis R. *Heavenly Chicago: The Architectural Tradition of Catholic Chicago.* Chicago: Liturgy Training Publications, 2005.

Miller, Donald L. *City of the Century: The Epic of Chicago and the Making of America.* New York: Simon & Schuster, 1996.

Monroe, Harriet. *John Wellborn Root. A Study of His Life and Work.* Park Forest, IL: Prairie School Press, 1966. Originally published in 1896 by Houghton, Mifflin & Co.

Moody, Walter D. *Wacker's Manual of the Plan of Chicago.* Chicago: Henneberry Company, 1915.

Moore, Charles. *Burnham of Chicago: Architect, Planner of Cities.* 2 vols. New York: Da Capo Press, 1968. Originally published in 1921 by Houghton Mifflin Co.

Morrison, Hugh. *Louis Sullivan: Prophet of Modern Architecture.* New York: The Museum of Modern Art and W. W. Norton & Co., 1935.

Nickel, Richard, and Aaron Siskind, with John Vinci and Ward Miller. *The Complete Architecture of Adler & Sullivan.* Chicago: Richard Nickel Committee, 2010.

Pardridge, A. J., and Harold Bradley. *Directory of Apartments of the Better Class Along the North Side of Chicago.* Chicago, 1917.

A Portfolio of Fine Apartment Homes Compiled by the Michigan-Erie Office of Baird & Warner, Chicago. Chicago: Baird and Warner, 1928.

Pratt, Richard. *David Adler: The Architect and His Work.* New York: M. Evans and Co., 1970.

Randall, Frank. *The History of the Development of Building Construction in Chicago.* Champaign, IL: University of Illinois Press, 1999; originally published in 1949.

Roche, R. Samuel, and Aric Lasher. *Plans of Chicago.* Chicago: Architects Research Foundation; distrib. University of Chicago Press, 2010.

Salny, Stephen. *The Country Houses of David Adler.* New York: W. W. Norton & Co., 2001.

Schaffer, Kristen. *Daniel H. Burnham: Visionary Architect and Planner.* New York: Rizzoli International Publications, 2003.

Smith, Carl. *The Plan of Chicago: Daniel Burnham and the Remaking of the American City.* Chicago: University of Chicago Press, 2006.

Solomonson, Katherine. *The Chicago Tribune Tower Competition: Skyscraper Design and Cultural Change in the 1920s.* Chicago: University of Chicago Press, 2001.

Stamper, John. *Chicago's North Michigan Avenue: Planning and Development 1900–1930.* Chicago: University of Chicago Press, 1991.

Stone, David. *Chicago's Classical Architecture: The Legacy of the White City.* Charleston, SC: Arcadia Publishing, 2005.

Thomas, Leslie. *Chicago Skyscrapers, 1871–1934.* Champaign, IL: University of Illinois Press, 2013.

Thorne, Martha, ed. *David Adler Architect: The Elements of Style.* New Haven, CT: Yale University Press, in association with The Art Institute of Chicago, 2002.

Van Zanten, David. *Sullivan's City. The Meaning of Ornament for Louis Sullivan.* New York: W. W. Norton & Co., 2000.

Wolner, Edward W. *Henry Ives Cobb's Chicago: Architecture, Institutions, and the Making of a Modern Metropolis.* Chicago: University of Chicago Press, 2011.

Zukowsky, John, ed. *Chicago Architecture and Design, 1872–1922: Birth of a Metropolis.* Munich: Prestel, in association with The Art Institute of Chicago, 1987.

___. *Chicago Architecture and Design, 1923–1993: Reconfiguration of an American Metropolis.* Munich: Prestel, in association with The Art Institute of Chicago, 1993.

Zukowsky, John, and Jean Guarino. *Benjamin H. Marshall: Chicago Architect.* New York: Acanthus Press, with the Benjamin Marshall Society, 2015.

Zukowsky, John, and Martha Thorne. *Masterpieces of Chicago Architecture.* Chicago: The Art Institute of Chicago; and New York: Rizzoli International Publications, 2004.

SPONSORS

John B. Murray Architect
WWW.JBMARCHITECT.COM

fig. U1

fig. U2

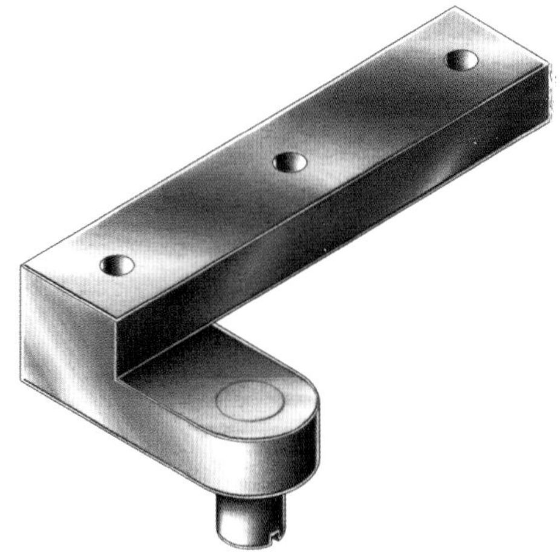

fig. U3

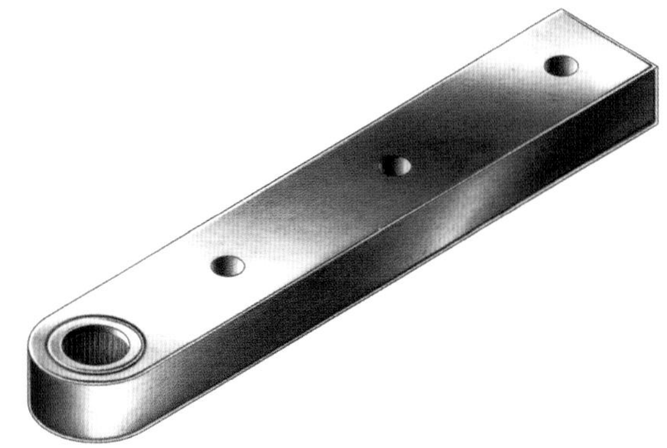

fig. M1

fig. M2

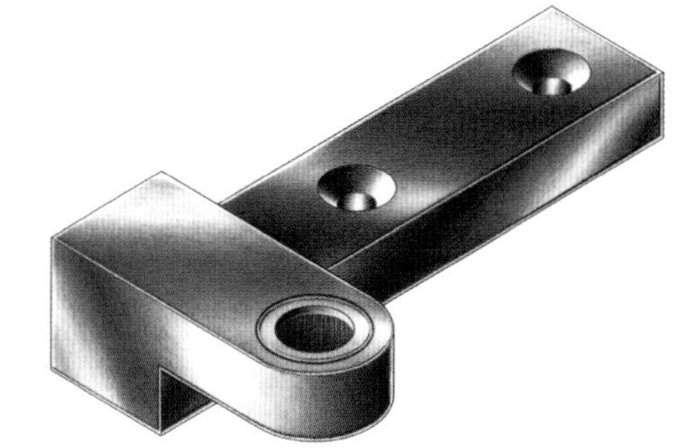

fig. M3

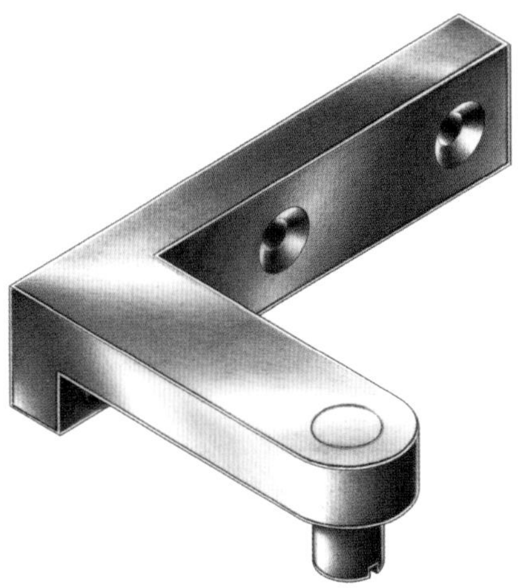

fig. U4

fig. U5

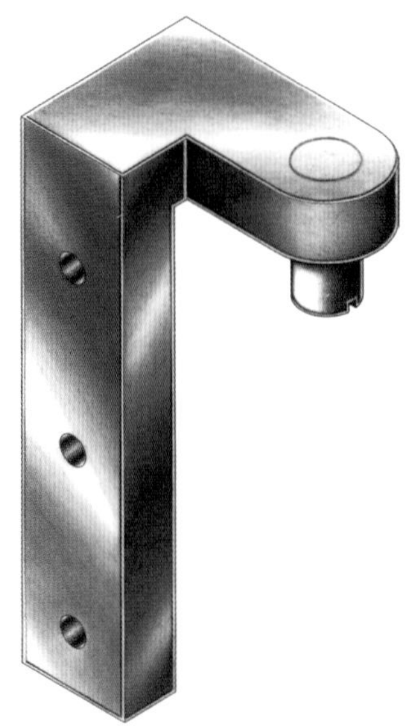

fig. U6

fig. M4

fig. M5

fig. M6

UPPER PIVOTS

Also Known as Header or Top Hinge Leaves

MIDDLE PIVOTS

Also Known as Door Hinge Leaves

E. R. Butler & Co.

Heavy-Duty Offset Pivot Hinges

The offset pivot hinge is an integral part of our legacy: it was sold by Ostrander and Eshleman, and manufactured, like the Harmon hinge, by the W.C. Vaughan Co. (Both companies have since merged with E. R. Butler & Co.)

In the specification of hinge configurations, offset pivots offer many advantages: a seemingly endless variety of mounting options, greater concealment, and an infinitely adjustable pivot point. Offset pivot hinges are ideal for concealed or jib doors, as well as built-in furniture and cabinetry. As with our other heavy-duty hinges, we have enhanced the traditional design to increase load capacity and reduce wear by adding full complement drawn cup needle roller bearings, thrust needle roller and cage assemblies, and thrust washers for all door and panel conditions.

Projection from pivot point to back of hinge is a primary consideration: it is variable and must be specified. E. R. Butler & Co.'s heavy-duty offset pivot hinges are made to order from 1 × ½ inch extruded material. Offset pivot hinges are available in all standard, custom plated and patinated finishes.

"CITY HALL PIVOTS"

Pattern Board for the New City Hall, Boston, Massachusetts

The W.C. Vaughan Co., 1967–1968

E.R. Butler & Co. Research Library, W.C. Vaughan Co. Archives

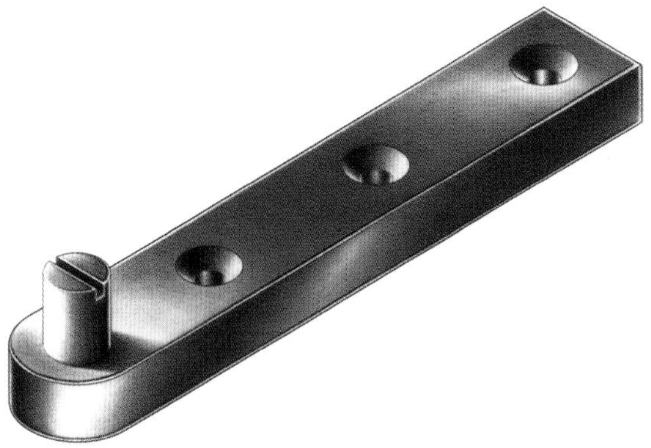

fig. L1

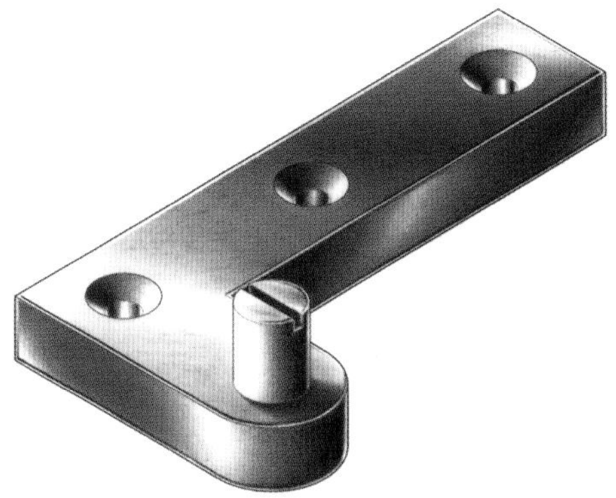

fig. L2

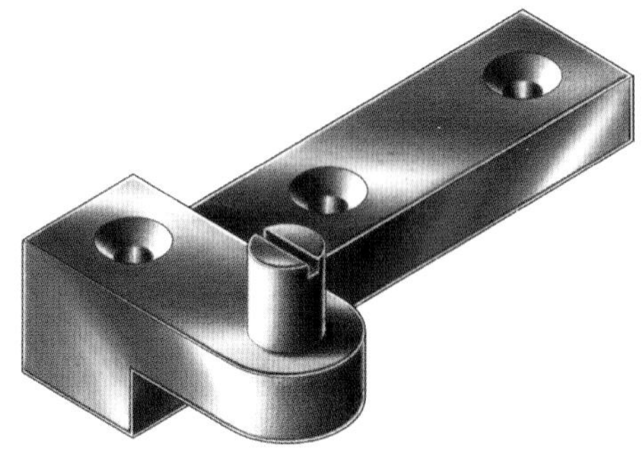

fig. L3

fig. L4

fig. L5

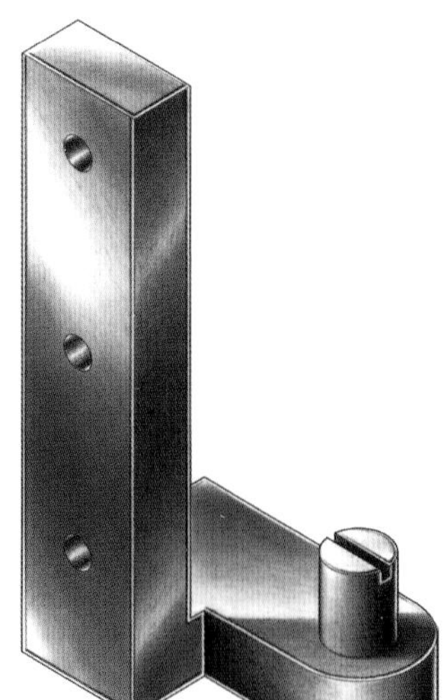

fig. L6

LOWER PIVOTS

Also Known as Sill, Floor, or Bottom Hinge Leaves

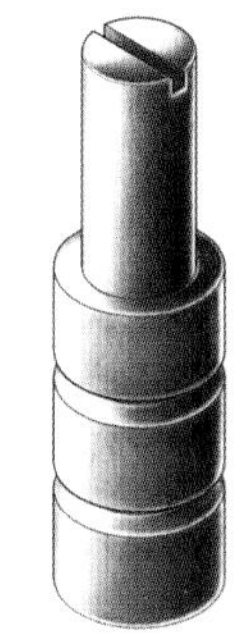

fig. S1

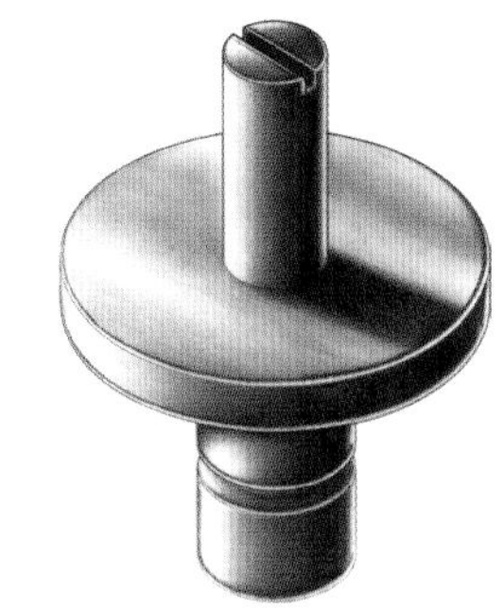

fig. S2

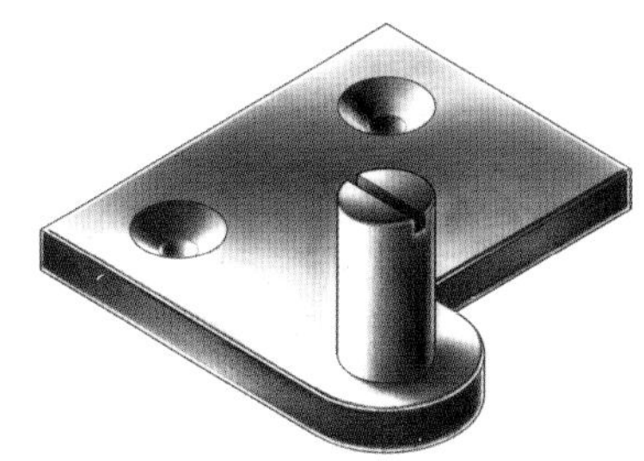

fig. P1

fig. P2

UNIVERSAL PIVOTS

Also Known as Studs or Plates

½ Scale

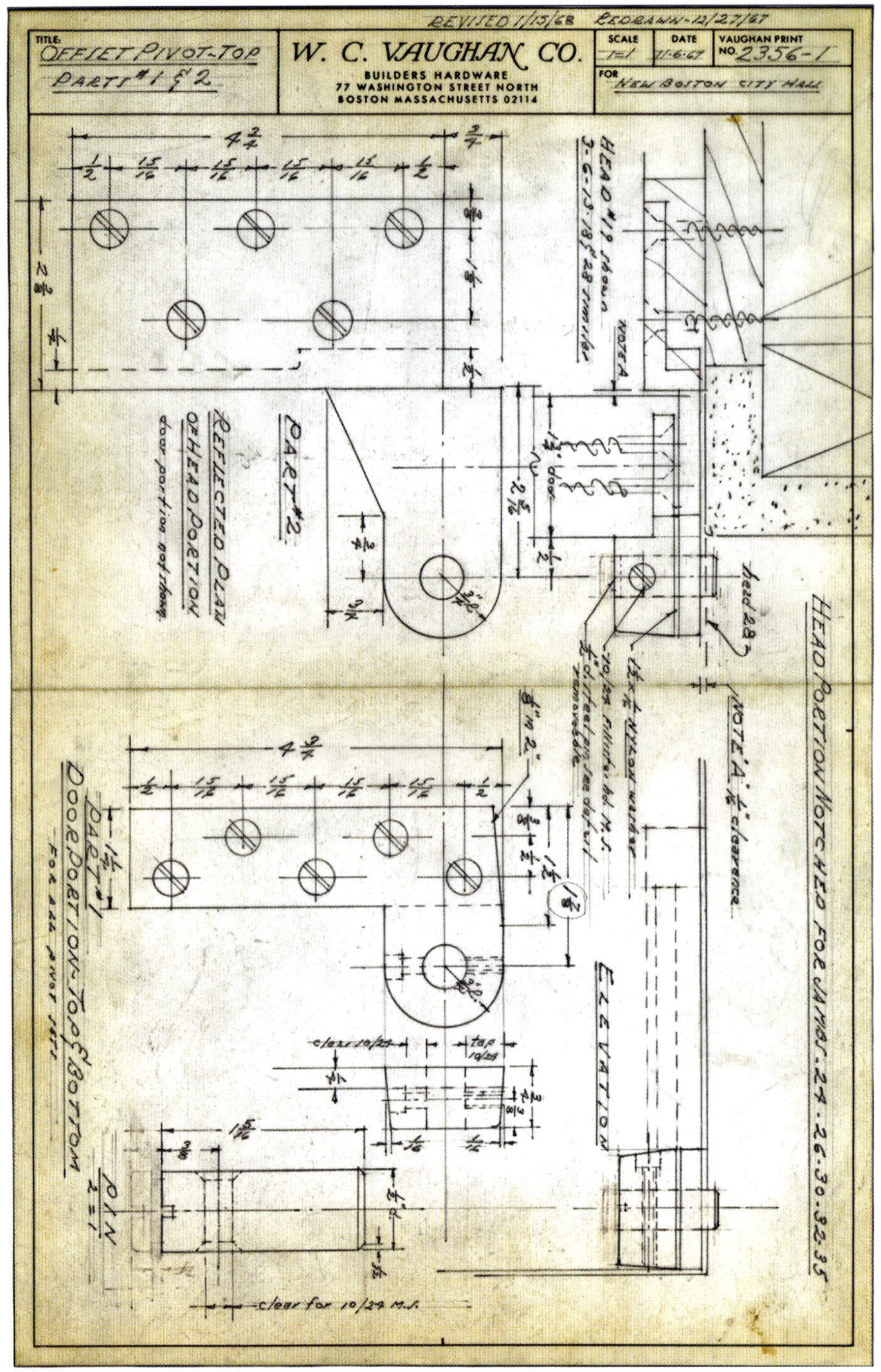

"OFFSET PIVOT – TOP PARTS # 1 & 2"

Drawing No. 2356-1, for the New City Hall, Boston, Massachusetts

The W.C. Vaughan Co., 1967–1968

E.R. Butler & Co. Research Library, W.C. Vaughan Co. Archives

E.R. BUTLER & CO.

MANUFACTURERS

WWW.ERBUTLER.COM

CATALOGUES AVAILABLE TO THE TRADE

SHOWROOMS BY APPOINTMENT ONLY

Technical Drawing: John Sykes Fetterman

FERGUSON &
SHAMAMIAN
ARCHITECTS, LLP
TELEPHONE: 212-941-8088
www.fergusonshamamian.com
Photo: Lisa Romerein
BOB DYLAN
Anselm Kiefer
Miquel Barceló

Doyle Herman Design Associates
LANDSCAPE DESIGN
D H
D A
DHDA.COM | 203 869 2900

HARRISON DESIGN
ARCHITECTURE - INTERIOR DESIGN - LANDSCAPE ARCHITECTURE
harrisondesign.com
ATLANTA LOS ANGELES NAPLES NEW YORK ST. SIMONS SANTA BARBARA SHANGHAI WASHINGTON, D.C.

Photo by Mike Kelley
ERIC J. SMITH ARCHITECT
5 UNION SQUARE WEST, THIRD FLOOR, NEW YORK, NY 10003 | 212 334 3993 | WWW.ERICJSMITHARCHITECT.COM

ONG-ARD ARCHITECTS

Architecture & Planning

Project Architect - Olivia Rowan, Photography - Durston Saylor

PETER PENNOYER ARCHITECTS
PPAPC.COM
Photography: Eric Piasecki

JOHN DERIAN
FLOWER
CONSTRUCTION
FLOWCON.NET
(908) 219-4102

BULLEY & ANDREWS
Proud builder and admirer of beauty, harmony and proportion since 1891.
bulley.com | @BulleyAndrews

LIEDERBACH & GRAHAM, ARCHITECTS
WWW.LIEDERBACHANDGRAHAM.COM

KANE
— DEDICATED TO EXQUISITE LANDSCAPES —
KANEBROS.COM

LUCIEN | LAGRANGE®
STUDIO
LUCIENLAGRANGE.COM

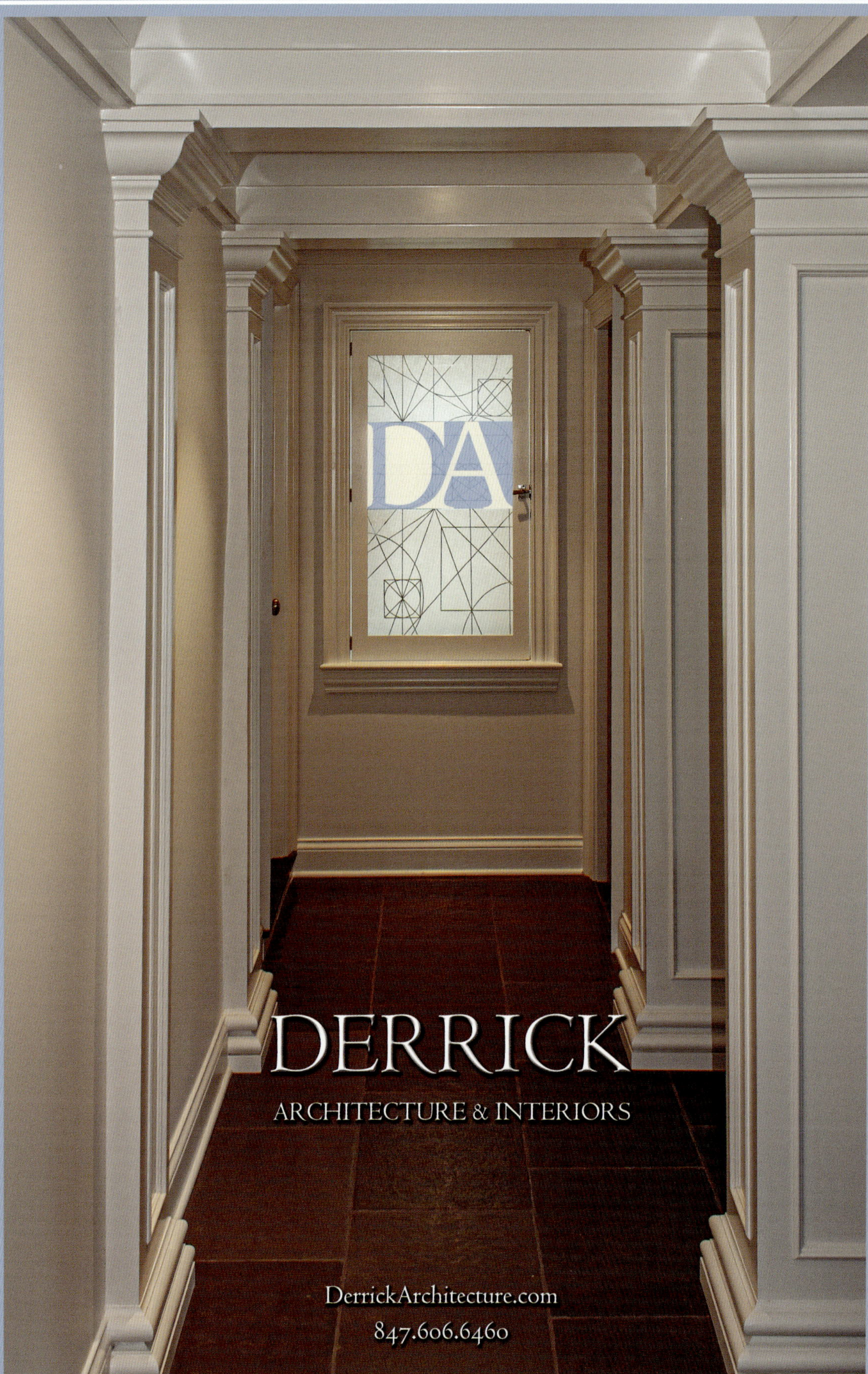
DA
DERRICK
ARCHITECTURE & INTERIORS
DerrickArchitecture.com
847.606.6460

THE ART OF FINE GARDENING
CRAIG BERGMANN
Landscape Design, Inc
design | installation | garden care
847.251.8355 | www.craigbergmann.com
Pictured: French Mediterranean Gardens, 2016 Acanthus Award Winner in Landscape Design

118 Bay Avenue, Huntington Bay, N.Y. 11743
Phone: 631-424-0905, Fax: 631-424-4867
E-mail: info@gcmw.com
www.gcmw.com
GOLD COAST METAL WORKS
- New York - Olomouc

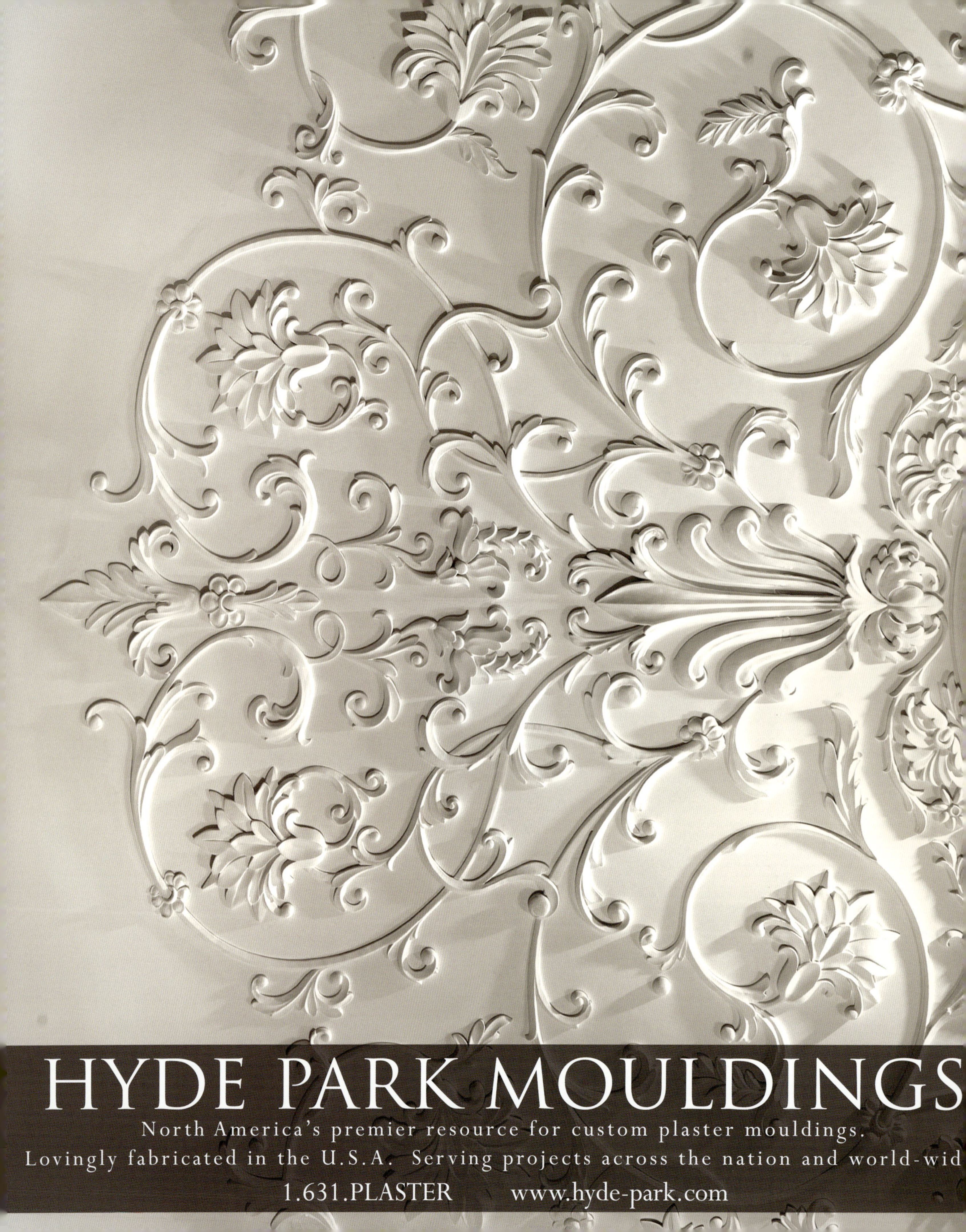
HYDE PARK MOULDINGS
North America's premier resource for custom plaster mouldings.
Lovingly fabricated in the U.S.A. Serving projects across the nation and world-wid
1.631.PLASTER
www.hyde-park.com